Escape Route to Ecstasy

Ida Byther-Smith

McClure Publishing, Inc.

Cover Design by Kathy McClure

To order additional copies, please contact:
McClure Publishing, Inc.
www.mcclurepublishing.com
800-659-4908

Dedication

I dedicate this book to my two grandmothers, Ida Mae Sutton-Lee, and Frankie Mae Smith-Robinson. They both always said, "Never say what you won't do! Just say what you haven't done!!!"
Life is a funny thing.

Pleasurable

To my wonderful, loving children, James, Melissa (Artis), Lavinia, and Branden, along with my grandchildren, Addie, Alex, Aaron, and Ashley. You are my hope, my dreams, my source of love and laughter; you are my joy ... my life.

Richard, for the happy years, some of the best years of my life, and the memories I will treasure forever.

A special thanks to THE MILLIONAIRE'S CLUB AND FES. You have made a big difference in my life.

Acknowledgement

Eugene Davis, you would not let me give up. You were persistent and continued reaching out even when I did not want you to!
Thank you.

Introduction

Meghan Kramer, a woman in her late thirties, found herself in the middle of making a decision that could change her life for the better. Her past haunting her like a splinter in her finger that she cannot see but can feel the pain going deeper and deeper inside her skin. As much as she wanted to move on with her life, the more her past keeps coming back to haunt her.

Meghan's first husband, Wade, her children's father, who was a great man was good to her. However, the relationship did not work out. After separation and divorce, she eventually meets Nick Kramer. What she thought she was getting was not what she expected. Years later, their relationship dissolved. *What's left?*

A woman who have been married twice with four children feels like this is it. Getting into another relationship would be a waste of her time and will seem like torture. It would put her back where she was after her first marriage ended. Getting to know someone else new would be starting over again. Who wants to start over? *No one.*

As Meghan was going on with her life, work and home life, everything was well. She still felt like there was another part of her that needed to be awakened. Although she has adjusted to this life and had gotten to a routine, something life changing happened.

She meets a new friend. This man wooed her. He taught her things that she had never experienced. It was exactly what the doctor ordered.

Tyler staring into her eyes as if he were trying to look into her soul.

"Meghan, the only thing I want to know right now is if you still love me."

Standing tall and ever so slender with his muscles protruding through his light blue shirt, Tyler continues to stare deeply at her, into her eyes. With a few moments of silence, Meghan still did not speak. Tyler's expression fell and his countenance changes. It was as if he became a different man.

If only she could put her feelings into words. How could she say what she wants to say and what she needs to say?

My God, she thought to herself. What will Tyler do when or if I tell him? What will he say? Will he leave me? Will he feel dirty and feel as if I did it to him?

Meghan found herself wishing that she could take a bath in bleach, hoping that would make her feel clean again. She felt filthy inside and out.

"Tyler"—Meghan stood with her back toward him—"you know I love you, but...."

Her voice was almost inaudible. She just could not face herself, or face Tyler, and tell him what had happened, not yet anyway. She could hear her mother's voice in her head, saying, *God will not put anything on you that you can't bear.*

Well, she was thinking to herself, *God must think I'm Wonder Woman … because this is a hard pill to swallow*!

Meghan's mind trailed back for a split second to what seemed like a lifetime ago—back to a remote place in time when she was overjoyed and happy. It was all because of Tyler being in her life. She thinks, *would he leave out of my life once he finds out?* Almost as if recovering from a coma, she snaps back. NOW THIS! Her feelings swipes away from the joy of that faraway time and her mood changes to anger. She is mad as hell—but at whom? What had given rise to the anger? How had this happened to her?

Tyler was trying to make small talk, but she was not listening. She needed to be alone; she had things to think about.

". . . .Tyler, I----I really need some time alone. Will you grant that to me?"

He nodded affirmatively, and added, "Yes baby, of course … take all the time you need."

Even in his sensitivity, his face expresses hurt and disappointment, obviously wanting to know more.

He left, and the moment he was out of her sight, Meghan begins to cry, wailing in pain as if she were dying. She suddenly felt like she thought any Thirty-six-year-old woman would feel. The pain had become too much to allow her to face reality.

In order for her to shed some of the burden, Meghan decides to go for a drive, but what would be the destination? She drives toward the lake, a place where she would always find serenity. While driving, it feels like she would never get there. Tears rolling down her chicks dropping and landing in her lap like puddles of water after a storm. The aching pain inside her soul is unbearable that she feels like giving up.

As soon as she parks the car, she walks to the shore barefoot holding her sandals in her hand. Standing and watching the waves coming to shore and going back, helps Meghan remove the thought of death. She just wants to think back to the good times. *God, I wish I had someone to talk to*, she thought. But there was no one, only herself. She feels so alone.

Meghan's thoughts travel to a remote place and begin to remove the negativity. Her mind travels back one and a half years prior to a blissful place.

ONE AND A HALF YEARS PRIOR

This was when the best thing happened to her since she became a mother ... the night she met Tyler Scottsdale—the man that she may have just pushed out of her life forever, but she knows he was the man she would love forever.

It was only one week into the new year, and Linda, her sister, is getting ready for work and decides to call Meghan.

"Meghan, come on girl, and come to the club tonight. It will do you good to get out of this house."

"Yeah, right. Lyn, I have told you before, I love my life."

"Is that what you call it? Life!" Linda shot back at her. "Girl, start the year out right. Get out. Have fun!"

Meghan sighs. "Okay, you win. I will come up there about ten tonight, but if some man comes up to me acting a fool, I will leave in a heartbeat. So, do not come after me if I leave. Okay?"

"Okay, just come," Linda said, running out the door in order not to be late for her second job.

Meghan cooked for her children and went to lie down for about an hour. After she got up, she took a long bath, and made sure she took extra time with her hair and make-up.

After four kids and two husbands, she still looked very good, not skinny, but like Laila Ali, Muhammad Ali's daughter, the boxer. She must say that at 5'9", and about one hundred and eighty-five pounds, she still looks very good! If there was one thing Nick Kramer did, it was making her aware of her assets. He always told her she was a real woman, not that she knew what that really meant, but it was nice to hear.

After getting the kids settled down, and homework out the way, she was just about ready, when Mark, her teenage son, comes in. "Mom, are you going out?"

"Yes, I thought I would go up to the bar where your Aunt Lyn works."

"Good, he said." He had been saying for a while that she should get out more, and have a social life. "Mom, all my friends say you are fine!" She just smiles; she knows this is true because his friend Steve has said it to her, but she dare not to tell Mark. He would go off on Steve for saying such things to his mother.

"Do you think you can watch your sisters for a few hours?"

He gives her that look—the one that says, "Mom, I'm NOT a child. I am sixteen years old."

"I know, okay."

"Thanks. I'll be back around two o'clock. Make sure you'll be in bed by one o'clock."

She would let them stay up a little later on the weekends, thinking that was only fair. They needed their down time too. After one last look in the mirror, she could not understand why Nick wanted out of their marriage. He said he still loved her. What was wrong? Well, this was not the night to dwell on it.

One of Linda's friends, Alice, had stopped by Meghan's house to give her a ride to the bar. When they walked in, Meghan felt as if all eyes were on her. Linda looked up with a big smile.

"Hey, hey, Ms. Meghan in the house!" Linda shouts over the music. By this time, all eyes were on her. Men were looking like scavengers at how desirable Meghan looks, and women were looking as if they could kill her. She sits at the bar and orders Crown Royal on the rocks, with water back, which was her choice of liquor. About three guys tried to buy her a drink, but she politely refused each. She learned a long time ago to BYOD (Buy Your Own Drinks). That way there wouldn't be any misunderstanding when she was ready to leave. She would be in debt to no one.

Alice, who drove Meghan to the bar, had met up with a male friend. She told Meghan that she would have to get a cab back home, with a wink! As Meghan sat there listening to the old sounds of 60's music, sadness creeps over her, but she was determined not to let Linda see her pain.

After about an hour, she told Linda she was going to get a cab and go home. "Oh Meg," Linda asked, "give it a few more minutes why don't you? Will you wait till I get off?"

"Are you kidding? I got to check on my kids."

"Meg, you know Mark is going to take good care of his sisters. Just stay a little longer."

"Okay, but twelve a.m. I'm out of here."

About ten minutes later, Red, Linda's man, walks in with this fine guy behind him. Linda was smiling.

"Wow! Mr. Scottsdale! What wind blew you in here?"

"I just came to have a drink with Red. He wouldn't take no for an answer, but you know I'm in my car, so I can leave when I get ready."

"Well guys, I want you to meet my sister."

Red said, "Hi, Meghan. I get to put a face to the voice." This was his first time seeing her. The extra time Meghan took with her dark brown shoulder length hair and makeup gave her a radiant glow.

"Yes, how are you, Red? shc responded. Tyler Scottsdale was just looking at her as if he were ready to take her home but was trying not to look so obvious.

Before Tyler knew it, he says, "Damn Linda, where have you been hiding her?"

Linda smiles. "She doesn't get out much, or I should say, not at all?"

"Boy, I'm sure glad she is out tonight!"

"Don't get so happy. She was just about to get a cab home."

"Not as long as I got a car," replied Tyler.

Meghan looked at Linda and rolled her eyes.

"Girl, he is a very nice guy. Plus, he is my supervisor. Please don't act a fool with him."

"I don't care, he is still just a man," Meghan said with a voice cruel as a new knife.

Linda looks at Meghan and asks the guys what they were drinking. Red spoke first, "You know I'll have a beer".

Then it was Tyler's turn. "You know the only thing I drink is Crown on the rocks."

Meghan looks up. He had gotten her attention at that point. *Anyone that drinks Crown could not be all that bad.* "What are you drinking Meghan?" Tyler asked?

"Crown Royal, and I buy it too! I only drink Crown on the rocks water back."

They both laugh. Well, he said, "Now I know we have something in common."

Linda places everyone's drinks in front of them. Tyler could not keep his eyes off Meghan. She was sneaking looks at him also. Meghan was thinking that if she could order a man, Tyler Scottsdale would be the one. He was about 6'2" 210 pounds, light brown skin with dark brown eyes that seemed to look right through her. He had a beard lightly salted with gray in it, not much, just enough to look distinguished. *DAMN this man was handsome.* She knew he had to have a woman or was married. He could not walk around single looking that good.

They started talking to each other, sharing information about themselves. He had been driving buses for the city for thirty years. Out of the blue, Tyler unexpectedly states, "Girl, you look so good I could kiss your daddy!"

"Well, he is no longer breathing among us."

"I am sorry. But I would have liked to thank him because he knows he made you for me."

Meghan smiles. "I bet you say that to all the girls you see in the bars."

"Well Ms. Meghan, I don't go to bars that much. So, I can't say that to all the girls" Tyler said sorely.

She could see he seemed to get a little steamed. She wanted to change the subject at that point.

"Now Mr. Tyler, you don't mind if I call you Ty?"

"Why not, everyone else does." He was sounding much calmer.

"Okay, then Ty it is."

"Look Meghan, bars are not my cup of tea. So, why don't we get out of here. I will take you home."

Meghan looks at Linda for approval. She got it with a nod of the head.

"I hope you don't get me shot."

"Meghan before you walk out with me, I want you to know something. I am married, but in name only. I could take you home with me." By that time Linda was listening. She looks at Meghan, and again she nodded her head.

"Take me home with you!" You got to be crazy."

"Yes. Take you home with me."

"Everybody knows their own shit remember that."

She knew her sister would not put her in a dangerous situation. So, she let him take her hand and lead her out into the night. After they were in the car, he asks if she would like something to eat.

"You know I could go for salad and a burger."

"Okay, we will go to Jordan's. They have good steaks."

"I love steaks."

"Unless you got some place else in mind."

"No," she smiles, and Tyler drives in the direction toward Jordon's. Once parked, she waits for him to open the car door. He did just that, and he reaches for the door to the restaurant and Meghan steps to the side.

Inside, the maître d' asks what table they would prefer. Their choice was a very good table in a secluded corner. Soon the waiter came, and they knew exactly what they wanted and ordered their meal. Tyler let Meghan order first. Meghan is impressed because most men she knew want to place the orders.

"Meghan, I meant it when I said I was married in name only."

"Why did you get married, Ty?"

"All my friends were doing it. She was my teacher at the time, I was seventeen she was twenty-two and had a good future ahead of her."

"What year was that?"

"In 1958," he said.

Meghan had to stop and think while glancing at him, *I was only six years old at the time.*

"I was dating a high school student, and had left her to start dating the teacher who was more experienced."

"How much more experienced?"

"She did things to me that I had never experienced. Girls my age were not that experienced. At least the one I was dating."

The waiter brought their food. She blessed hers silently and said, "Amen." They began to eat in silence, sharing little to no conversation. But each time, she would glance over at him, and he was watching her. She became self-conscious to the point that it was almost impossible to chew her food. He was generating heat within her just from how good he looks. She could feel even more heat radiating from the depths of his eyes each time he looked at her. She tried not to look over at him, wondering what was going through his mind.

The chemistry between them was electrifying. He was attracting her like a magnet. The desire she had for him was growing stronger, no matter how hard she tried to fight it.

"Would you like dessert?"

She raised her head and met his gaze.

"What?" She seemed to be partially in a daze.

He smiles, "Dessert."

"No thanks, I'm full."

After a little small talk about what they do for a living and Meghan shares about her four children, she wants to be sure he knows about them and not be surprised later.

"Okay I'll take you home now. Do you want to take the rest of your meal home?" looking at the amount she did not eat.

"Yes, I would. Thank you."

Neither was big on wasting food. She would enjoy the food later while eating alone. He asks the waiter for a carry out before paying the check, and they soon left.

The night was still young, and the light breeze blowing in the night air causes Meghan to walk slowly to the car. She wants to show Tyler that she is interested without expressing it in words. Her body language mesmerizes him. It was almost hypnotic.

As they were driving home, she was surprised he knew her address. As if he was reading her mind,

"I was with Red once when he dropped Linda off, but I had no idea you were inside. If I had known you were in there, I would have come in without knocking."

She smiles. "Okay. Ty, let me tell you something. You don't have to say things to make me feel good."

"Meghan just remember one thing, I don't have to lie to you, that is why I was honest with you before. I'm 48 years old, and no one is going to get me for lying except God." I am serious. Linda never mentioned you.

As they neared her door, she asks if he would like to come in for a drink?

"What about the kids?" he asked.

"It's about two o'clock. They should be asleep by now plus they are on the third floor."

The house had three floors. That was one of the reasons she bought it. Linda has the basement apartment, and the rest belongs to her and the kids.

Mark even turned the attic into a getaway for himself.

Meghan had made it perfectly clear to him that if she ever caught a girl up there, … so long to a private spot. But with Mark, she knew that would never happen. Mark and his mother had an understanding never to lie to one another. Before anything got to the point of no return, they would talk about it.

She unlocks the door, and they step inside. It is dark except for a light in the hallway, which she keeps on at all times. She takes his hand and leads him through the darkness across one room, then passed the kitchen to the family room. She turns on the light. Tyler is following close behind her.

She went to the kitchen and then to the bar, to which only she and Linda had keys. She poured two glasses of Crown and returned to give one to him. He sat down and she turned on the music box. At that moment Teddy Pendergrass was sounding so sensual with "Turn off the lights," which she loved. She sat beside him.

"Do you need more ice?"

"No, I'm fine. Let's dance."

He was standing by this time, with his arms out toward her. She slid into his arms as if she belonged there. Perfect fit! He was holding her so tight until she had to put forth some effort in order to breathe. This reminded her of high school. As his grip got tighter those aches between her legs became more noticeable to her. She was afraid he was going to notice that her body was going into a trance. She tried to act cool, but her body had a mind of its own, and boy was it going crazy! The last thing she should be doing was dancing so close to this man. *We just met*, she thought.

God help me, was another thought that ran through her mind. His manly scent was causing the lower part of her body to moisten. She could tell he was enjoying inhaling her scent also as he takes in several deep breaths. She could not even pretend to be drunk, not at all. She was as sober as a judge. Besides, Tyler was not the kind of man that would take advantage of her if she were drunk.

She blinked when he pulled back and caught her licking her lips. The depths of his dark eyes gazing back into her light brown eyes, turned gray by now and caused a hot flame to burst from within as if what were dead had come alive. If nothing else, this proved there was sexual chemistry between them, regardless of the time or the place. And, who knew when they would take one step further and make love. Meghan could feel it coming. There was no doubt.

He wanted to tell her that he had not felt this way in years. *Would she believe me*? He thought. He had paid for the sex he had in the past twenty years, but this with her was something else. This was a different feeling and unexpectedly. It was really beyond belief. He could not bring himself to tell her. What would she think if she knew he paid for sex! Meghan was the kind of woman men would give anything to be with just to sit and talk with her.

Tyler would pay a million dollars just to dance with her, but he knew that would make him or any other man hated by her. She was the kind of woman you wanted to be with forever. Her husbands must have been damn fools. One day he would ask what happened, but this was not the night. He just wanted to be with her caressing her body.

"I feel hot," she said. Her voice was breathless and husky in a way he had to notice.

"Then let me cool you off," was his reply.

"Cool me off or make me hotter?"

He only shook his head and smiled before saying, "I'll let you be the judge of that."

NO TURNING BACK!

He was removing her blouse while she watched him, unable to do anything about it, and not wanting to. His gaze was intense, intimate, and hot. After tossing her blouse aside he unsnapped her bra. Her breasts poured out before he could get the bra off completely, and he felt the perspiration forming between the twin globes. She shimmied out of her skirt to give him a hand. There she stood wearing only black lace panties. He suddenly made a sound. She heard the low growl that radiated from deep within his throat. She slowly unbuttons his shirt, licking her lips as his strong chest appeared. It was then that he undressed quickly as she was helping him!

And then in a deep, husky, desire-laden voice he said her name, "MEGHAN!" Her legs became weak. She could barely hold herself up, she was at his mercy. Suddenly her entire body felt so weak she had to reach out and grab hold of his shoulder to keep from falling. He pulled her panties down as he kissed her stomach and then her thighs. She picked her feet up one by one helping him remove her panties completely. Her clitoris started throbbing.

"If we're going to stop, now is the time." His words touches the flame within her; suddenly this made her crazy with desire. With her eyes closed, he pulled her to the couch as if he were guiding her to a great surprise. He started kissing her all over her upper body twirling his tongue around her nipples gently sucking them then working his way down her body. He starts making love to her like she was the meal he needed to survive.

He stopped just long enough to say, "I need to have my way with you. I want you, Meghan, I want you. I need you."

She wanted him to stop talking and keep working on her before she started thinking this was wrong. Again, she thought, *we just met.*

Meghan was about to lose her mind. She had spent half her life praying for a man to love her until she got enough. But before she could draw her next breath, he was kissing and licking his way up her inner thighs again. His tongue invaded her, doing double duty. He was both torturing and satisfying the ache in her body again. She almost lost consciousness, but he would not let her.

"Stay with me baby," he moaned.

The sensations that tore into her were too sharp, too electrifying for her to do anything other than enjoy each moment. She held on as he relentlessly devoured her, licking, and sucking, as sensations shot all the way through her bloodstream. She felt the explosion again and tried to push him away before it happened, but his hand was firm, possessively cupping her back as he continued twirling his tongue over and over.

She moaned, "Tyler!" She had to put her blouse in her mouth trying to muffle the moaning sounds. At the same exact time she felt her stomach constrict, she had begun to experience feelings that swept through her total being. These feelings were so strong, so totally out of her control that they had her almost screaming. It was like nothing she'd ever felt before. Her body began vibrating between her thighs and she found herself pushing hard against him, instead of pulling away.

It took some doing, but sensations began ebbing and her body was slowly being pulled back into a different gear, maybe. There was a heartbeat of silence. Then she heard Tyler say huskily, "Get ready baby, we've barely got started."

Not letting him totally take over, she sat up and said, "No baby, it's your turn." She had to let him know he was not in this alone. She took a swallow of her drink, and set it on the table. It took her a minute to get it together. Now she was ready to show him what he had been missing in his life also.

NOT A LITTLE GIRL!

She started kissing him with strong lips at first. Then her kisses got very soft, kissing his eyes, nose, lips, and chin, all the way down to his nipples. She could tell from his reactions he really liked that. So, she spent a little more time there. She wanted him to know she was not a little girl, but a full-grown woman. Then she licked his navel with long strokes.

He was lying there with his eyes closed calling her name, playing in her hair. She was glad she did not cut it last week. He was enjoying every minute of this.

"Baby! Where have you been all my life?"

"Right here, honey, waiting for you to find me."

As she worked on him, he could only think this was some of what he had been deprived from even as a married man. This was the kind of woman he needed and wanted. He wonders *if they were married would she change like Betty did*. He hurries and put those thoughts out of his mind. He just knew he was going to do everything he could to keep her from now on. Her tongue was moving, licking, meeting in a private sensual and heat-blistering dance to the soft smooth jazz music that was playing.

He wanted to wrench his mind back from all the erotic emotions she was making him feel, all the heated lust invading his body. Instead, he was being overtaken by some primal elemental force that sent vibrations of deep need all through his body. The air they were breathing seemed to change, and he felt his entire body begin to melt. The vibration was rhythmic. He heard himself surrender, and he felt himself being pulled more and more under the mastery of Meghan Kramer's grip. Then her hands moved back to his nipples, and she never stopped her action. Her fingertips caressed his breasts kneading their softness, playing, torturing, and tantalizing his taut tips.

He heard himself whimper when he became entrenched in desire so strong, potent, and deliberate that he could not breathe. She did not care that he was pulling her hair with such force that she was sure he would pull some out. The only thing that was important now was to finish what they started; any regrets could come later, but not now. She did not care! Something had taken over both of them, and had held them in a sensual grip. It was not something either of them could explain, nor did they feel they needed to, or did they even want to. It was enough that they both felt it. They both wanted it, and they both intended to have it.

"Meghan," he grabbed her and held her so tight until she had to ask to breathe.

As if he could not believe what just happened, this feeling, he kissed her and said, "I want you Meghan, I need to be inside you right now! Baby, please let me inside you." She knew right then she could not stop even if she wanted to. She also needed him to be inside of her. She pulled him down on her, only to realize he could not get in her.

"How long has it been?" he asked.

"Years. Push a little harder, I don't care if it hurts. I need you now! I want you in me now." Tyler put his finger in at her portal until a gush of liquid covered his fingers. Holding him in her hand, Meghan swung her body up to his and he slowly eased into her. She had him completely inside her. Moments and minutes increased in time. Tyler is a man with deep passion and knew just when to reach her level of ecstasy. He looked into her face, pulled her face to his, and kissed her while her eyes were closed.

"Look at me Meghan, you are mine now, and you'll always be mine."

At that moment they both knew what they were sharing went beyond temptation. It went beyond anything they knew, and it would set the stage for the wonderful love they would always share together.

They had bonded, this man and this woman. They lay there together until their temperatures had returned to normal, each hating to depart from the other. But she would not ask him to spend the night. He would not have stayed if she asked. She had children to raise.

"I hate to leave you," Tyler said. "I wish this could last forever."

"I do too. Ty, I want you...." He stopped her.

"Don't say it. I'm man enough to know you don't do this with everyone, I know better than that! You get some rest. I will call you by the time I think you are home from church."

She answered, "I do go to church every Sunday, and tonight won't stop me from going tomorrow."

"Pray for me."

Meghan had already made up her mind to pray about moving forward with their relationship. There is no turning back now.

"How does dinner sound after you get home from church?"

"Will this be like a real date?" she asked.

They both smiled, and he kissed her lips.

"I look forward to it."

She walks Tyler quietly to the door and sighed before saying, "Thanks for tonight." Then he left.

She went upstairs, checked on the children. The girls were in their beds as usual. She knew Mark was fine, so she did not check on him.

She took a bath and went to bed. Meghan was asleep as soon as her head hit the pillow. She slept better than she had in years.

Meghan was awake by 8:00 a.m. Yes, five hours of sleep. Ever since she trained and drove the bus for Cage, she could only sleep five hours at a time. It was a habit that had lasted for years. Today was no exception. By the time the kids got up there was a complete meal, and she was on her second cup of coffee.

The look on their faces said it all. "What's up mom?" Tina said. Meghan knew there was a smile on her face. This time it was real, not just there to make the children feel good. She was happy.

Mark spoke, "It's good to see a real smile and not a phony one." Leave it to Mark to notice almost everything. She had not felt this alive in years. Linda came upstairs, and took one look at her smile and Meghan's eyes said so much more.

After the kids were off to get dressed for church, she walked over to Meghan in a low voice to make sure the kids didn't hear.

"Where did you go last night when you left the bar?"

"If you must know we got something to eat and came home."

Meghan was hoping Tyler would not say anything to Red; she did not want to hear Linda's remarks about her behavior on the night before. She knew Linda did not see Tyler's car because he parked in the back of the house. Linda was never going out back that time of night for anything, not even for a fire.

"What time did Tyler leave?"

"We had a drink MAMA if you must know." Linda was overprotective of her, even though Meghan was older.

"If you must know I got my five hours, I slept very well."

"Good, you need to get out sometime and have a few drinks. It will do you good, and will make you feel better."

After the small talk, Meghan and the children were off to church; she learned long ago Linda was not going. So, she stopped asking.

True to his word Tyler called around 4:30p.m. "Hi, Meghan."

"Hello Tyler!" By the tone of her voice Tyler knew Meghan did not expect for him to call. She did not believe he would call after last night.

"You sound like you are surprised to hear my voice."

"Well...."

"Look Meghan, I really enjoyed last night, and I'm not about to let you walk out of my life. The only person that will get you away from me is God, and my arms are too short to box with him. Understand?"

"Yes Ty, I understand."

She was wondering why, *after he got all the cookies last night, he would call*, as she smiled to herself. She thought, *he was a man not a boy*! She really did not expect him to call, but she was happy he did.

Tyler picked Meghan up and was dressed to the *hilt.*

When he rang the doorbell, Meghan opened the door. She looked at his 6'2" well-built lengthy body from head to toe and asked, "Is that an Armani suit?"

"It sure is. How did you know?"

Not giving him the answer. Meghan indirectly says, "I love a man in a nice suit"—while staring at his upper chest. Tyler had his shirt part of the way opened. He was not wearing a tie.

"Well, I will have to dress up more often."

She glanced at his shoes and thought, *Those are Armani shoes. This man is going to make me fall deeper in love with him.*

Tyler trying to get her attention. "Meghan, you look lovely."

He grabbed her and hugged her so tight while taking deep breaths. Her fragrance was inviting. She had freshened up and touched up her makeup wearing the same dress she wore to church. It was a fashionable light blue dress that could be worn on any occasion.

"I see we are matching."

"Yes, how did you know I was wearing blue?

"I did not. I wear dark blue suits more so than black."

"Let me get my purse."

Tyler said as Meghan got loose from his bear hug, "You sure smell delicious."

"Oh Tyler, you need to stop before we have to detour and go to dinner later." She laughs.

As they were walking to the car, Tyler held her close beside him with his arm around her waist. They both walked as if they were walking down the runway. He reached for the passenger door and Meghan saw 'TS' on his cufflinks. She was really impressed that she did not have to tell him how to dress. He had style and charisma.

This time they decided to go to Gibson a seafood restaurant. The chef prepared their meals just right.

"This steak is so tender," Meghan stated.

As Tyler cut into his lobster tail, he says, "This lobster is fresh and cooked just right."

Meghan liked her baked potato loaded with extra toppings while Tyler only liked rice pilaf with his meals. He is not big on potatoes.

This time their conversation was different. It was as if they already had all the answers, they needed to know about one another. They had already been intimate, so they did not have to pretend. The mood was relaxing leaving them wanting each other even more.

After the main course, Tyler asked if Meghan would like to see a movie. "I hear Fatal Attraction is a great movie to see."

"Yes, Michael Douglas is staring in that movie. I enjoy seeing Michael Douglas."

"Me too."

"You're not a fatal attraction, are you?" Smiling while asking Meghan. She asked him the same question. They both just laughed.

They decided to share desert. The waiter brought two spoons. As they were scooping the whip cream from the apple caramel whipped pie, Meghan just had to show him some tricks with whip cream. They sat in a secluded area in the restaurant to feel more private.

The waiter appeared out of nowhere. Tyler asked, "Can you bring us the check?"

"Sure."

"Dinner was nice, Tyler. I certainly hope we get to spend more time together. I haven't done this in a long time."

"Meghan, I am going to show you what you have been missing. I want to fill every void in your life."

Meghan went to the lady's room to freshened up before they left the restaurant. When she returned to the table Tyler asked, "Are you ready, baby?"

"Yes."

While watching the movie, they could see areas where relationships can go wrong. Every time something happened, they would both look at one another and smile.

After the movie, they decided to go for a ride taking the scenic route. As much as Tyler wanted Meghan, he knew he did not want to make it seem as if he only wanted to have sex with her.

He took her home and kissed her good night at the door. She was happy how Tyler handled the evening. This made her feel really good, knowing last night was not just about sex.

Monday was a very good day. Tyler called her at work, "I hope it's, okay?"

"Yes, I never get calls or anything, unless it's the kids."

He was taking notes, studying her likes and dislikes. He wanted to learn more about her. He told Meghan he did not want to wear out his welcome, so he made a date for the following Thursday night. He knew she loved B.B. King, and he had tickets to the show that night at The House of Blues. He wanted to take her. This was the first time he had met a woman that shared his interests to the extent that she did.

He thought it would be nice to send flowers to her job on Wednesday, just around the time they were getting ready to change shifts and leave for home, flowers were delivered.

Meghan was at the time clock when Judy, one of her coworkers, ran in the back. "Meghan, there's someone out in the lobby asking for you."

"Who is it? The patients and staff know I'm out of here by this time of day."

"It's not a patient or staff," Judy stated.

"Oh hell," Meghan said, turning to go to the lobby. Who in the devil could it be? She just wanted to get out of there. Besides, her feet hurt. Meghan was hot and sweaty. She wanted to get home and get a bath before cooking. Walking toward the lobby, Tyler crossed her mind.

She was stopped in her tracks by the delivery man, who was holding the flowers. But he gave her the card first. The flowers were so lovely. She could only smile, a beaming smile. All eyes were on her. That bunch of beautiful flowers seemed to brighten the day for everyone, and was the subject of much pleasant conversation.

"Man, someone must think you're very special." Ms. White, the p.m. charge nurse was saying with a big smile. "Boy, I wish someone would send me flowers just for no reason on a Wednesday!"

The card read, "Just for being you, Love TYLER!"

"Is there something you want to tell us Meghan?" Judy asked.

"No. I just got to get home," she stated with a smile. He had really made her day and she would call him as soon as she got home, and got herself together. She still could not believe he did this!

After getting her bath she paged Tyler, and he called her back. "I was really surprised today, just as I was getting off work," she said.

"I'm glad you like them. I hope you understand how I feel, Meghan. I love being with you. Please believe that I will do anything for you. Just tell me what you want me to do!"

"Tyler, I went into this with my eyes wide open. You never lied to me. I would never put pressure on you. I like you also, but you know my father was always unfaithful to my mother, and I said I would never be a home wrecker!"

"Meghan please don't feel bad, you didn't pull a gun on me. I'm the one to blame, if there's any blame to be given. I'm the one that's still married. I will not apologize for loving you. Meghan just say it, and I'll leave now if you want me to!"

"Ty, please don't ask me to say something like that to you. We really don't know each other that well."

"I know all I need to know, Meghan. People like us get together once in a lifetime! Let's just go for it."

"I could never live with myself if you left Betty. Ty, as much as I love being around you, I could never ask that of you. But I do love you! Now I understand what my grandmother meant when she said, 'never say what you won't do, and just say what you haven't done. Life will make a *lira* out of you.' Tyler, life will make a believer out of you. If I ask you to leave Betty, someday you will hate me."

"I wouldn't let this turn into hate."

"Ty, I don't think you understand the feelings I have inside for you. I know it will never ever change. I now know what LOVE feels like!"

"Meghan that's what I've been trying to tell you ever since the first night I was with you. Girl, if I died right now, I would die a happy man knowing you were mine for a night.

Meghan, I now know what it feels like to be in love! I have never ever felt like this before! Meghan, I met a woman, a woman that's on the same page as I am. Is it possible for you to meet me around 6:00 pm? We need to talk; just about us and maybe then we will understand each other better."

She meets him at Valois Restaurant on 53rd at 6:00 pm. After finding a seat they got right to the point.

"Meghan, ask me anything you need to know about me. I want to know everything about you!"

"Ty, what could you want to know about me that you don't already know?" She asked.

"Well," he said, "what is your favorite color, foods; music, also other likes and dislikes so we can get on with our lives, and we will be together forever baby!!!"

"Forever is a long time," Meghan replied. "Can we talk about the forever part tomorrow? I really can't say forever tonight."

"My favorite colors are white, black, red, blue, purple and green. Favorite music are the blues, R&B and Country."

They talked continuously for two hours while eating, and then Tyler took Meghan home.

THE NEXT DAY

Meghan thought about Tyler most of the day at work. She really enjoyed spending time with him and felt anxious about seeing him again.

After work she had just enough time to cook for the children, take a shower and get dressed. Mark made a comment, "Mom are you dating?"

Meghan stopped and asked, "Is that okay with you all?"

All four spoke at once. "Mom, we would love it if you got out more, we want you to date! Can we meet him?" It seemed as if they had rehearsed.

"Not just yet, give it a few more weeks, okay guys?" "Okay mom." Rachel spoke first. Nicole and Mark just kind of shrugged their shoulders, Tina just looked at all of them in agreement by saying, "It's cool," and that was the end of the subject.

Looking at the clock, Meghan had just enough time to make it to the steak house they had agreed upon.

Tyler was there waiting for her. Meghan liked that because she was always on time. If she was late something was wrong. As a matter of fact, once when Meghan was in training with Cage, she got a ride that caused her to be late. The instructor was about to call the police to report a missing person when she walked in. Meghan said then she would always travel alone if possible. That way she knew that she wouldn't be late. Quite the opposite, she would be early. Early was on time and on time was late to her.

Tyler stood as Meghan approached the table; he pulled the chair out for her.

"This should tell you something about me." Yes, she thought. *He's quite the gentleman*, and then thought of *his love for steaks too*. He had spoken of how hard it is to mess up a steak. She had to agree with him, and they both laughed.

Each one had learned two things about the other. They both loved eating steak. And they both loved being on time, never late.

"Well Meghan, tell me what foods you like most. I know you like seafood and steak, but what other foods are your favorite?"

"Well now, let me think,"—rolling her eyes, thinking—"I like all food! Seafood is my favorite. I can say there is not too much I don't like as long as it's cooked. I don't eat raw meat that cannot walk or talk." They both smiled at each other.

"Meghan Kramer, tell me more about you. I know you told me some, but I feel there is more to know. Your hobbies, sports, and don't leave anything out."

Tyler could listen to Meghan talk all day. Her voice was not too deep, and her pitch was not too high. It is a smooth voice with the right tone.

"Well Mr. Scottsdale you know I have four children, Mark, Nicole, Rachel and Tina. We spend time swimming together throughout the year at an indoor pool.

"My hobbies are fishing, drawing, writing, sports, and traveling. I love to play basketball and softball." By this time, he was looking at her with disbelief in his eyes. She had to stop and ask, "What's wrong?"

"You must have named everything that I love. Are you for real?"

"I think I'm real."

"How often do you do any of those things?"

"Not much. I fish with my children, and I belong to a club at the YMCA for the rest. This is where I get a chance to do the other things I like to do."

"What about you?" Meghan asked.

"I get to travel some, my daughter, June, goes with me sometimes, but Betty and I have not been any place together in twenty years. I tell people all the time she has a son, and I have a daughter."

"Okay tell me more."

"Ms. Kramer, I had given up on everything except Crown Royal until I met you. There is a God! I don't want you to feel bad about anything that happens between us. I will never disrespect you in any way, and I will be in your life forever if you let me. I'm not a rich man, but I know you have wants and needs. I will try to meet most of them. Is that fair enough?"

"Yes, it is." Meghan made up her mind right then and there this would not be a sex only relationship. They would have fun and enjoy each other with no strings attached. Meghan was not looking for another husband. The past few years had been HELL on her and the children. Mark had asked if she would not get married again, until he was out on his own. This was not the kind of relationship she had hoped for, but it would do for now.

Months went by, and they were inseparable. He took her everywhere. They went to dinner anytime and anyplace, without any worries. He was right. He was married in name only. As a matter of fact, it had been so long since he had been out with his wife, or another woman, that most people thought Meghan was his wife. He acted as if she was too. The only thing Tyler knew that Meghan did not know was that Betty was dating someone that she bowled with every Thursday night. For some reason, he just could not tell her that, but Linda and all the people at work knew this had been going on for over twenty-three years. Andrew, Betty's boyfriend, even went by their house every once in a while.

June had come home from school and walked in on her mother and Andrew once. June told Tyler and he relayed June's information to Betty. She did not deny anything, and she seemed to be okay with the truth.

What kind of man would Meghan think Tyler was, if she knew this? The truth was Tyler really didn't give a damn about what Betty did, but Tyler knew it would be different with Meghan. Since he met Meghan, he liked the way his life was going. How long would Meghan put up with this if she became free? Hell, she was free. They just had to get the divorce. Meghan had told him once that she had no plans to ever get married again. Nick had taken a lot out of her, but neither of them would sign the papers.

Tyler could not believe the way he was thinking about this woman. Was he losing his grip? They got along so well that people did not know they weren't married. It seemed as if they could read each other's minds. Tyler was at all of Meghan's job events, and she was at his also.

Tyler invited Meghan to an event on his job and he won a trophy participating in the bus rodeo drive. He presented the trophy to Meghan. He was so happy that she got a chance to see him behind the wheel.

One evening Meghan's job had an all-white party, and they were looking like angels dressed in white. Tyler wore white jeans and a white shirt leaving nothing to the imagination. He was blessed. Some of Meghan's co-workers noticed too. One said, "You are looking fine in all that white." She noticed all that black in all that white, and do not think that the men did not see Meghan's 44 Ds in that white dress too.

After being together for two months they planned a trip to Mississippi for a week. She had talked with Linda, who was all for it. Linda would supervise the children in Meghan's absence. The children and their aunt all knew the rules to be followed, and there would be no disobedient behavior.

Tyler was also concerned about the care of the children while their mother would be away with him. He thought it was time to go to his hometown to see his family and introduce them to this beautiful woman. Not only was she good to look at, but she was also a beautiful soul, from the inside to the outside.

Packing the car with their luggage then hugging the children before leaving, set the trip in motion. Meghan had included bottled water and made sandwiches in case they got hungry part of the way.

As Tyler was driving on the way to Jackson, Mississippi, Meghan becomes very flirtatious. She starts playing with his ears and her hand moved down to his inner thigh.

"Don't build a fire that you can't put out."

"Who said I cannot put it out."

Meghan starts unbuttoning Tyler's shirt and his chest protrudes out. She rubs his chest in a circular motion.

"I'm driving. I am driving."

"Just hold the wheel."

Now, she unbuttons his pants, and Tyler is thinking *what is going on*. This is something he has been thinking about most of his life and here is a woman that he is not even married to is about to fulfill all of his high-way fantasies.

Although Meghan would not stop messing with Tyler, he looks around at the trees on both sides of the road and looks in his rearview mirror to see if anyone else was near especially 18-wheelers because he knew the drivers would be able to see inside the car if Meghan keeps going with this.

And, at that moment, he felt GLORY!!! And the glory that he felt made him hear music in his ears.

"If we have an accident, your head is going to be in my lap."

"Don't worry. I am paying attention. You should keep your eyes on the road."

"How could I?"

CLARKSDALE, MISSISSIPPI

Soon after arriving in Clarksdale, Mississippi, Tyler's hometown, Meghan meets his brother and sister-in-law. Right away, Meghan could tell Fran did not care much for her. Fran made sure Meghan and the rest knew it. Fran was the type who would look down on other people. Tyler had warned Meghan that the woman was a real 'BITCH' to put it mildly.

Meghan was not going to let anything spoil this trip. They had not been together sexually since that first night at her house, and she was ready! They both had agreed the next time they were together it would be in a bed with no distractions from anyone or anything. It was hard to maintain this with just a few kisses and petting, nothing hard because they both were trying to hold out for the right time. There were times when she really had to push him out the door. She would have to run and take a cold bath. This is what it took trying to hold out, and they would laugh about it when they were alone. For the first time in years, she really felt alive.

"Well Ms. Meghan, what kind of work do you do?" Fran asked, with a smirk on her face thinking,

If you work at all. That was Fran, always assuming she was better than another person.

John just looked at her, then at Tyler. He knew Tyler cared very little for Fran.

Meghan, well prepared replied, "I'm a nurse. I work in dialysis. Also, I'm one of the charge nurses in Nephrology at Mechanize in Chicago."

Even Fran knew that was the best hospital in Cook County. John sat up in his chair with a smile on his face.

"What's your profession Fran?" Meghan asked.

Fran looked shocked, and said, "I teach school."

"That's good". Meghan responded. "We need good teachers. I have a B.A. in Education, but with things like they are now, I went back and got my master's in nursing."

Tyler could tell by the look on Fran's face she did not expect that. John and Tyler knew Fran could not compete with that. Fran knew she only got through college because John knew the Dean. In addition, John only married her because she told him she was pregnant, only to find out that was a lie. They were married eighteen months before Connie was born.

Everyone in town knew John Scottsdale was and always would be in love with Maggie Walker. He had confided in Tyler that Fran had pictures of him and Maggie together, and she would show them to every soul in town if he tried to leave her. John didn't have the heart to tell Maggie. He just let her think he was what they call 'hen-pecked' or that he was in love with Fran. John could never let Maggie get hurt. John also told Tyler he hadn't touched the woman in fifteen years. As he put it, he couldn't get drunk enough to have sex with Fran ever again in life.

Sitting on John's patio outback away from the women, John made Tyler take a long look at his life. Tyler did not hate Betty, but he knew for the first time he would walk away from everything for Meghan if he could be with her for life. After thirty-one years of marriage, he was really in love at forty-eight years old, and he would be willing to start over in a heartbeat. Tyler wondered, *what reaction Betty would have. Would she feel the same way as him, that this was a marriage for convenience only*?

John asks, "Is it the male menopause, bro?"

"Hell no, this is real," was Tyler's response. "I went through that twenty-three years ago around the time I started drinking like a fish. Now I have two or three drinks and I'm good, with her or alone. Sometimes we sit and talk for hours. We get along so well until sometimes I'm afraid I will wake and find out that it's just a dream. John, you only get one shot at this! I want to enjoy her."

"What if Meghan wants to enjoy more someday?"

"You know what man. I will give it to her. I will start over in life for her."

"I know what you mean. If only I could turn back the hands of time." Tyler could see the hurt in his brother's eyes and understands.

Meghan walks from the kitchen to the patio her voice brought Tyler back into the present moment.

"Earth to Tyler, earth to Tyler, are you with us?"

He grins at her. Meghan's eyes and smile could melt his heart. Just looking at her made him want to do things he had not thought about in years.

"Well bro, we are going to have to go if we want to be in Jackson before it gets dark." Besides, he had enough of Clarksdale. They said their goodbyes and got into the car. Both of them noticed the look in John's eyes. He looked sad, as if he wished he were leaving with Tyler and Meghan.

* * *

JACKSON MISSISSIPPI

They made good time, arriving in Jackson about 7:00 pm. It was time to check into the Holiday Inn, and by the time they got everything in order it was 7:30 pm. Checking her watch, Meghan knew her grandparents were in bed. "Let's just get a bath and something to eat. We will get an early start in the morning," she offered.

"Okay," Tyler agreed. They both got a bath. She was first. Then while he was taking a shower, Meghan called Linda briefly to let her know they had arrived safely. She talked to the children also to let them know she was fine. She made it a point to compliment them on the positive reports given by their aunt Linda. Then she called her aunt Jess to let her know they were in Jackson at the hotel. She would see them in the morning. After hanging up Meghan knew everyone would know within an hour. Aunt Jess was the one to get any message out to everyone.

By the time he walked out the bathroom she was fully dressed. He walked over, took her in his arms and kissed her long and hard. Their tongues played inside each other's mouths. "Get dressed," she said, pulling away from him. "I need food, man!"

"Okay I will feed you woman!" They both laughed. Normally, they would go to a steak house, so Tyler asked the desk clerk about a nearby steak house that served good steaks.

"Are there any great steakhouses in the area?"

"Yes. One about two miles east of here."

She recommended a particular one. It turned out to be a very nice place. After they were seated, Tyler ordered a steak with a bowl of clam chowder soup and a grilled chicken salad for her. That was Meghan's request.

"Are you sure that is all you want to eat?"

"Yes. It is somewhat late. I will have more for breakfast, I guarantee you," she replied.

After an hour or so, they went to the bar on the other side of the restaurant. They danced a few times to the slow jams. Then they both decided to go back to the hotel. Tyler paid the tab and they left.

Back at the hotel, Tyler picks her up, unlocking the door at the same time and carried her into the room. After standing her on her feet he stated, "I have not had a kiss in hours. No, it honestly seems like days!"

Her eyes were taking in the site of his body, now in his open-collared shirt. Even through the shirt she could see the six pack. His tight trousers emphasized his muscular legs. He was in better shape than a man half his age. She swallowed hard as she told him not to rush.

"Man, you smell so good I feel like eating again," she said. Meghan could tell the comment pleased him.

"You always say things to make me feel great." Tyler walks across the room and got two glasses, and a bottle of chilled champagne. She looked at him with wondering, childlike eyes. There was no champagne in the room when they arrived. "I ordered it while you were taking a shower since neither of us has to drive tonight."

"Let's not kill the entire bottle," she suggested. "You, at least, should stay sober."

"Why?" Both his eyebrows shot up as he caught the bubbles with a towel. "I can take that a lot of ways."

"Sure, you can," she said, making herself comfortable on the gold-colored comforter on the king size bed, smiling. "But you are a clever man! You know what I mean."

"Really." Tyler poured champagne into each of the long-stem crystal glasses. "I hope I'm clever enough not to make any mistakes with you."

"I don't imagine you will, none so far."

Tyler clicked his glass with hers. Meghan patted the place beside her on the bed, "Sit here with me."

"Are you sleepy?"

"Me? Are you kidding? Sleep is the last thing I want tonight. Meghan, I want you with every breath I take. I want you like I never wanted any woman. Tyler put his glass on the bedside table and reached down to flip on the radio.

"Let's dance." Luther was singing, and was halfway through the song. But Tyler did not care. He just wanted her in his arms. The look in her eyes said the same. Nonetheless, she remained seated on the bed mesmerized. He was standing before her with his legs apart, and a lover's smile on his face. His masculine aura had overwhelmed her.

The next love song came on. He reached out and pulled her up into his arms. She sprang into his arms, and laid her head against his shoulder, eager to let him lead her wherever he wanted them to go.

"Are you nervous?" Tyler asked.

"No, I am not nervous." But Meghan did not believe her own words. Tyler stopped dancing.

"Baby, why are you trembling?" Only two months ago the passion in her body that had been hidden for years woke up and Meghan was feeling like a real woman again. If there was one thing she had, it was a high sex drive. You might say it ran in the family. Meghan spent a lot of time praying to God to keep hers under control, but now she was alive. She wanted to love, and she wanted to be loved. God, she needed this man. It had been a long time since….

"Please don't ask me any questions." She moved closer to him and kissed his neck. He bent his head, tightened his arm across her shoulder, and traced the seams of her lips with his tongue.

She needed more, much more. He began to stroke and move against her with the rhythm of his body. This gave rise to something in her. Now, a wild, wanting desire possessed her. She slithered against him, moving to his beat. She heard her own moans of frustration, and didn't care. "Kiss me," she said. "Tell me what you want." She unbuttoned the jumpsuit exposing to him her firm round breasts.

"Oh baby!" He lowered his head, covered her left nipple with his warm mouth, and began to suck as if his life depended on it. Hot darts danced in her belly and flowed down her thighs until she felt an unearthly heat boiling in her vagina. Groaning from the sweet torture of his biting and sucking, she reached down and stroked him.

With his head thrown back, and teeth clenched, he let her have him. She stroked and squeezed until he cried, "Stop baby, or it will be over, before we get started."

"I thought you would like it," she whispered.

"I love it, and I love you."

"I just want us to take our time; after all we have all night."

"I want to take this thing off you!"

"There is a zipper in the back!"

Tyler had her out of her clothes, except her underwear within seconds. While turning back the cover on the bed, he stopped and looked around as if to see if he had forgotten anything. "Good Lord! You are beautiful!" Meghan's breasts nearly spilled out of her pink bra that was meant to shield only her nipples. When his hands went to her back to unhook the bra, she stopped him. She covered his hands with hers. Tyler stopped, picked her up, and placed her on the bed. She struggled to keep her hips from swaying as her body hungered for him.

"Don't be shy. I have waited for this ever since that night in your house two months ago."

She held out her arms to him. In only a moment he slipped out of his clothes and got into bed. She peeled off his shorts and started kissing him all over his body.

"Honey, no more of that right now."

He removed the bra and sucked her breast again, but when Meghan began to toss and turn in desire, he left it and kissed her forehead, eyes, ears, nose, skipping her lips and went to her throat. She swung her body up to his, but he restrained her as her body throbs to his heartbeat.

"I want to feel you!" she said, "I want you inside me. Let me hold you! Let me hold you!"

"In a little while." His hot breath on her nipple sent tingles cascading along her limbs. She begin to moan as he sucks her nipple and strokes the other in double assault tenderly. Her nipples firm and respond as her breast standup at attention.

"Please Honey, get in me!" she begs. He answers, letting her know he was almost ready.

"I will baby, as soon as you're ready."

"Ty, I am ready. I'm on fire!"

Nearly out of her mind with desire, she tried to take him into her hand and force him into her. But he moved, playing with her until frustrated beyond caring what she did. She raised her body to meet him. He plunged his tongue inside her cave and sucked, nipped, kissed, and thrust. This continued until screams poured out of her and she did not recognize her own voice.

"I'm so full I need to burst. Get in me Ty now! I want to feel you; I have to feel you NOW!"

"I will. It's what I want too, baby." He slowly crawled up her body. "Take me!" She guided him in her.

"Do you feel me? Oh! Talk to me baby!"

"Yes, I feel you, but I have this awful ache like if I don't burst, I will die!"

Meghan's body seemed to be on fire, and a surge began to crawl up her legs and thighs.

"Baby, do something, I can't take this! I am hanging out here." Rolling his midsection of his body counterclockwise while stroking and beating his manhood in and out of her deep cave rhythmically to the music playing. The sound of the music was coming from her clitoris.

"Oh God, I think I'm going to die!" Her thighs began to tremble. "What are you doing to me?"

"I am loving you, and you're not going to die."

Her inside began to swell. He was pumping her. She gripped it; she tried to steady herself by locking her ankles at his back, tightening her legs around him. He pulls out and starts kissing her moving downward licking her nipples then her naval until he got to her clitoris. He starts twirling his tongue while holding up her legs then sucking her clit. Meghan skirts a little come in his mouth. She had, had at least three orgasms already. He makes his way back up. His penis finds her vagina and makes its own way to the cervix area pumping like he wants her to reach her highest climax. All of a sudden, she could feel the joy and she could not stand it! She was drowning! Tears streaming from her eyes pass her ears falling onto the pillow as she looks up at Tyler.

"Ty Honey!" Oh, Ty!" Meghan flung her arms wildly and gave herself to him. He worked on her furiously, showering her with stars, giving her the sunrise, the sunset, and all the colors of the heavens until she burst wide open sexual groans and moans could be heard from a distance! "Oh Ty, that was so good! My! My! My! My! My! The ecstasy that Meghan reached was far beyond she had imagined.

Shouting his release, he gave her his essence and collapsed in her arms. He did not have the strength or the will to move. Locked in her arms, as well as her legs, he would willingly remain right there forever.

For the first time in years, the silence of loneliness he had felt with Betty in the past twenty years, did not plague him. He belongs to a woman who belongs to him deep in her heart. He'd felt it in every inch of his body, the minute she gave herself to him. Tyler knew his power of release did not come from his years of celibacy. It came from knowing that he was loved, and getting what he wanted for himself. And at the same time, he was giving her what she wanted and needed. Tyler raises himself putting weight on his elbow while starring at her beautiful skin glowing. "I love you Meghan," he softly and fervently whispered. She opens her eyes, smiles, and tightens her arms around him. His heart seems to slide down into his belly.

After about ten minutes, Tyler spoke. "Pinch me," he said.

"Why would I do that?"

"Just want to be sure that I am not dreaming. If I didn't know better, I would think I had died and gone to heaven."

Tyler brought his lips down on Meghan's. She opened her mouth and met him with a steaming kiss that said it all. "Meghan, the way I feel right now I will not be able to go back to the way it was."

She looked deep into his eyes, "What way was that baby?"

"I had given up on ever loving or being loved again in this life."

Meghan could see that faraway look in his eyes again as she did at his brother's house. She kissed him again very softly.

"I feel like a man with a woman that can make his soul sing again. I really cannot explain it, but I feel like I am whole for the first time in my life."

"I understand you, baby. I have a similar feeling," she said. "I had been celibate since my marriage broke up, not because men were not available. But after Nick's coldness and mood swings, I didn't want anything to do with men. I saw them and just looked through them. I just couldn't go through that again."

"You won't have to baby," Tyler said with a soft kiss.

He separates himself from her and lies on his side holding her hand.

Meghan sat up and looked at him. "Ty, you are a wonderful man, I have no regrets being with you."

If he only knew how great he made her feel.

At that time, he remembers the champagne. He rolls off the bed, reaches to get their glasses, fills them again, and hands her one.

"I don't have to stay sober tonight, do I?" Meghan lowered her lashes and pulled the sheet up to her neck.

"It's up to you. However, what will I do if I decide that I want some more?" she said in a little girl's voice.

Playing with him she saw a grin teasing his lips, "More of what? There won't be any champagne left!"

"You know what I mean," she said, pretending to pout.

"No, I don't have no idea. Tell me what you want, baby."

He took a long sip of his drink. "You had better do it soon because this stuff works fast."

"Well, maybe I will just lie right here beside you and suffer," she said. Laughter streamed out of her. She could not help it.

"Honey don't ever think that way. That should be the least of your worries."

"Man, when your engine heats up, you really heat up."

"Now tell me what you might want more of."

"It doesn't matter. You just finished off the champagne."

"Yeah, but I can still rock your world!"

She was feeling hot, and ready again. "Do you want more cheese and crackers?"

"Hell, no." He took the glass and put it on the table, joined her in the bed, and pulled the sheet down to her waist.

All he had to do was get one of her nipples into his mouth, and it was on again. He lowered his head and began to suck her right nipple soft just like she liked it.

"Tyler. Oh honey!"

He let his hand drift down to the apex of her legs, until she crossed her knees in frustration. He eased his hand until it cupped her middle.

"Are you sober enough, or do you want me to stop here?"

"Honey, please do not tease me, I was joking."

Then he felt her give in to him.

At that moment, he knew she had to have it all! Therefore, he lifted her, and kissed her. Excited by her moans and cries, he started feeling on her again with smooth tantalizing strokes that Meghan could not resist.

"Please, Ty." Meghan begged. "I cannot stand it."

He rolled over lying on his back pulling her on top of him. Meghan assumed he would love it this way. Besides, he was at her mercy.

"You want it? Take it," he said with devilish eyes.

"Do as you please with me."

He began to rub her nipples.

"Go ahead baby, it's yours!"

To his amazement she bent to his chest. All he could think was, man, this woman knows what she is doing. *Why couldn't I marry her today*? He thought. This was something that crossed his mind a lot lately. He knew he wanted Meghan to have his name. She did things to him and with him he had only thought about or saw in movies. Just that moment the sky came in on him. There was no holding back. He had to make a full deposit in her bank! It was just a matter of seconds before they both were sleeping in each other's arms. They had both put their time in and payday had come in full.

TIME TO MEET SOME FAMILY MEMBERS

The next morning Meghan awakened with Tyler sitting by the window watching her sleep. "How long have you been up? Is there something wrong?"

"I got up about an hour ago, and there is nothing wrong."

"You are lovely even while you sleep." Tyler walks over to where she was lying. He reached for her. Meghan put her hands up to her mouth. "Let me brush my teeth before you kiss me." They both laughed. Tyler loved that about her. She got up and ran to the bathroom, but left the door open enough to hear him talk over the running water, as she brushed her teeth.

"Okay young woman, who do we visit first today?"

"My grandparents."

He opened his eyes wide.

"Don't worry they will love you as much as I do."

"Did you say you love me?" This was something he was waiting to hear her say. She had said it before, but this time it was different!

"Ty, you know I love you!"

"I know you do baby. It just sounds good to hear.

How far are we from their house?"

"It's only about 30 miles south of here."

"Okay let's get started."

"Can we get something to eat first? You took a lot out of me last night."

"Yes, I don't want you telling people that I wouldn't feed you the morning after your whipping," he said jokingly.

They both laughed. You could hear the great time they are having with one another.

Meghan says humorously, "Yeah right!"

"Let me get a shower," She said, turning the water on.

"Can I take one with you?"

"Only if you keep your hands to yourself."

"Okay, I'll look at that fine body of yours." Ty wanted to get busy, but he maintains his cool.

"Can I at least wash you up?"

"Yes."

Tyler grabs the sponge and liquid soap. After Meghan rinses with fresh water, he starts washing her from the top down. She could feel how well he would take care of her. He was gentle in certain areas and slightly rough in other areas that she needed him to be.

As she rinses off the soap, she watches Tyler wash down with a smile on her face. He is an attractive man with a tight body. She reaches for a towel and hands one to him. She dries off and wraps the towel around her body.

Proceeding to get dressed, they both head out the door. Tyler walks with Meghan to the passenger side of his car and opens the door for her. They went to a nearby restaurant that served a good southern down-home breakfast.

After they sat at a booth near a window, the waitress sets two classes of water on the table and ask if they were ready to order, or did they need a minute. He orders orange juice and coffee for both of them and then orders Meghan French toast with bacon and scrambled white eggs. He really had a big appetite, so he orders pancakes, bacon, over easy eggs, and homemade fried potatoes with smothered gravy.

After breakfast, they arrive at a lovely house in the country one hour later. An elderly couple approaches the car. You could tell they were her grandparents. She looks like both of them, though they looked older. It was plain to see her grandmother was American Indian. Her grandfather was Black with skin as silk as a baby's butt. You would not believe he was in his seventies. Her granny, on the other hand, was a fine old woman with hair down her back parted down the middle of her head. Tyler could only think Meghan's mother must have been a very pretty woman. You could tell by looking at her parents. Tyler knew she died very young, Meghan said, from a broken heart. She would only say her father was a fool who died young also.

"Girl, it's so good to see you. This must be Tyler." Grandma Pearl said, excitedly.

Meghan introduced Tyler to her grandparents, and they exchanged pleasantries.

"I see you got a real man this time." Grandma Pearl let it be known that she did not care much for Nick Kramer. She had said once he was a "slick ass so-N-so with lying eyes." Granny would always tell Meghan, "The eyes are the window of the soul. Look at the eyes, and you will see the real person behind them."

Granny said Nick's heart was not right.

"Where are Linda and the kids, they didn't come?"

"No, Granny. This trip is just for us."

"Oh, you all on some kind of honeymoon?"

"Granny," Meghan smiled. She answers that the kids had camp and Linda was working. Linda is available for the kids, just in case I need her to supervise them while I am visiting family.

Meghan made it a point to clarify that this time was their vacation, and they were going to enjoy every minute of it!

"You're not glad to see just me?"

"Girl, you know I am always glad to see my oldest grandchild. Now hug me. They hugged each other warmly.

"Are you hungry? Want me to cook something to eat?"

"No, no, Granny. We ate in Jackson." Granny looks a little disappointed, she loves to cook, and she was good at it.

By this time, Grandpa Willie finally got a word in. "How are you doing these days baby?"

"You know me, Grandpa. I stopped complaining a long time ago." Grandpa had to smile behind that.

"Welcome son, come on in. Tyler, you want a beer?" He asked. "I got some on ice."

"Yes, sir, I'll take one. Meghan is driving."

Tyler went to the kitchen with him. Meghan and Grandma Pearl were talking a mile a minute. They had lots to talk about.

"Now tell me son, what do you do for a living?"

"I drive buses for the city."

"Oh, you must work with Linda."

"Yes, sir, that's how I met Meghan."

"Well, it's been years since I've seen my granddaughter so happy. Be good to her son, she is one of a kind. I will never let Pearl hear me say this, but Meghan is my favorite grandchild, and her mother was my favorite daughter. All of her family loves her. Meghan has a good heart. I am not saying it just because she is ours, but she really does have a good heart. Meghan took after my daughter...."

"What's taking you two so long?" Granny called out. "Your grandpa gets lonely around here with just me to talk to."

"Don't you keep him busy running after you?"

"Girl, stop it, with your fast self." Grandma Pearl and Meghan could talk about anything – even sex.

"He's old now," she said, with a big smile on her face, "but he's mine." Granny was still a hot mama, and everyone knew she would kill you if you messed with her Willie.

"Are the children all still doing well in school?"

"Yes, they are Granny. They seem to understand that school is their job for now."

Meghan and Tyler spent about six hours with them, and Granny even had a chance to cook. She prepared a fresh green salad, corn, and chicken, with iced tea. Tyler ate two plates full of food, which made Granny feel good. Tyler was right at home with them, and they fell in love with him.

"So how long will you all be here?"

"I only have a week off. So tomorrow we will see Aunt Jess and Carle." Jess was Meghan's aunt her mama's sister, and Carle was Meghan's sister. They had tried for years to get Carle to move north but she always said no. For some reason, Carle loved Jackson and as Linda would say, "living poor."

Meghan loved her sister and really wanted her to be happy. So, she never pushed her to move. After all, there were advantages and disadvantages of living in either place.

After saying their goodbyes, they went back to the city to get some rest. With the long day and big meal, they just took a bath and went to bed. Neither had any trouble going to sleep, wrapped in each other's arms.

They awakened about the same time ready to start the day, took a shower, and set out to visit more of her family. Aunt Jess loved Tyler and so did Carle.

When Meghan introduced Tyler, he gave both ladies a compliment about meeting them. He knew just what to say.

Meghan and Carle goes to the kitchen to get some of that down home lemonade while Aunt Jess and Tyler sat in the living room. Meghan noticed they had cooked a seven-course meal. She could really smell a southern down-home meal when she walked in the door. Little did Meghan know other family members were on their way.

Aunt Jess had already asked Tyler to stay for dinner because other family members wanted to see Meghan and it would be nice for them to meet him too.

"He is fine girl, and he seems to be so nice." Carle said.

Meghan could not say the same for Carle's man, Roger. Her husband had died and left her some money. Meghan felt that Roger was a leach. If Meghan had her way, Carle would drop the zero, and get herself a hero.

Aunt Jess said the same as Granny, "Girl, you got you a real man this time. He is the type of man you deserve, Meghan." She made sure to say it in front of Tyler, so that he would know she approves of him.

Once the other family members arrived, all of them sat talking about good times they had while Meghan, Linda, and Carle were growing up. Aunt Jess shared how they would interact with one another, excellent sisterhood.

The camaraderie amongst the family was delightful. Meghan laughed so hard that Tyler enjoyed himself too.

It starts getting dark, so Meghan suggest they leave before it gets too dark. Embracing her family before leaving, Tyler and Meghan heads back to the hotel.

That next day Tyler and Meghan decides to go site seeing. They both felt that this trip was exactly what they needed. After meeting Meghan's family, Tyler knew that the relationship is going in the right direction.

Heading to the Cedar Hill Cemetery Old Courthouse, Vicksburg National Military Park, and Vicksburg Riverfront Murals, the scenery was peaceful. Meghan shares memories of great times she could remember and loved ones she lost. She remembers going there for the first time in the sixth grade with Westside school. Her mom had mentioned that Meghan had uncles buried in the cemetery from war battles. On Sundays they would walk around the cemetery and read headstones. They just went site seeing for quite a while. They visited the National Cemetery in Vicksburg.

Afterwards, they went back to the hotel room. This time their desire for one another had increased. Tyler could not wait to get Meghan in the room. While in the car, she starts making love to Tyler using words that were enticing.

"Tyler, your thickness that penetrates my secret place causes me to moisten and drip all over you,—as she was rubbing his chest—just the thought of you being inside of me makes me hot all over again. Are you ready to give it another round?"

Tyler's mind was in a trance of ecstasy. He did not want to seem anxious because he wants to make love to Meghan not just get a quick one.

In the room, Tyler peels her clothes off piece by piece slowly while his tongue rolls around her ear and ear lope. He starts at the top slowly and moves downward to her clitoris. Meghan's moans were so romantically rhythmic that it was as if she was singing a love song from within. As Tyler's tongue was moving downward, Meghan feels he was rocking her world. *This could go on forever*, she thought. As usual, it was some good loving.

They checked out around 1:00 p.m. that Friday and got a head start back to Chicago. Meghan had to work ICU that Sunday night. Tyler had another week off. He was going to take some time fishing and asked Meghan if he could take the children.

Tyler and the children had so much fun together. It had gotten to the point that Meghan's children would miss him if he did not come over. Tyler took the time to play checkers and scrabble with them. He even took the time to take them skating on some Saturdays, and he never complained. This was not the type of relationship they had with Nick. Nick picked up on it when he visited. He was jealous of the type of relationship the children had with Tyler.

Tyler had her children so excited about checkers Meghan could not understand it. He taught them something referred to as English Draughts, which is similar to games that have been around for thousands of years. He even got all the game boards for them. He really had their attention when he explained the game dated back to 3000 B.C.E. Tyler references to these games were Plato, Homer, and Queen Hatasu.

"You have my kids hooked."

Tyler even went out and got all the kids their own skates. He was adamant about the children having their own skates because of feet fungus that might be in the borrowed skates at the rink. He would make it a point two Saturdays out of a month to take Meghan's children skating. He taught them all the moves crisscrossing, backwards, and spinning around. Meghan also learned more skating techniques. She hadn't skated in a while.

REQUIRED PHYSICAL

Tyler and Meghan had been together a year when Meghan got the news that everyone on the job had to get a health checkup. The medical facility tests were TB, HIV, and Hepatitis and anything else the doctor could name. Meghan was first in line that day.

"Let's get it over with, so I can get back to work. I have a date tonight."

"Girl, you ought to marry that man." Evette said. One of Meghan's co-workers.

. . . ."I can't—Meghan hesitant to say and then she says—Nick won't pay for the divorce." She never said Tyler was married also. With all the blood work, it would take two weeks to get the results back.

One night Nick stopped by to see the children unannounced and found out Meghan was out on a date. It slipped out of the girls' mouths. He did not know with who. He became upset and furious and did not express this to the children. Nick called her blackberry in his car and left a voice mail. "Why are you not home with the children? Call me!"

Meghan was so happy, Nick seemed jealous. He came around a few times and made the statement that she was running wild.

She returns his call to let him vent. When he left her, she lost everything. He got a lot of nerve telling her what she should be doing.

"You need to keep your ass at home with your kids!"

"You're not staying home," Meghan said sternly, "so why should I? I am a grown woman, and I pay my own bills. You need to take care of your own business."

Nick was hanging out a lot over to Meghan's and had brought his roommate with him once or twice when he found out Meghan was dating. She did not care much for his roommate. He gave her the creeps. He would just stare at her and Tyler. Tyler called him 'the creeper.'

"That's your ex-husband's roommate?"

"Yes, I don't like that dude! I guess he is okay, but I really don't know him well enough to make any kind of judgment one way or another about him."

Meghan never would say much bad about a person even if she did not like them. Her mother had taught her that if she could not say something good about a person, not to say anything at all. Nick claimed they shared the bills.

D-DAY (LIFE IS NOT FAIR)

Two weeks to be exact from the date of Meghan's blood work, Meghan was sitting around drinking coffee when the phone rings. "Mama, it's for you!" Rachel called out, before getting into the shower. Bell, her supervisor, was on the phone. "Hey girl, what's up?"

"Meghan, you don't need to come in today you have to go over on Clyde and see Dr. Robin."

"Dr. Robin, who is...."

Bell did not give her a chance to say more. "Just go to 9212 Clyde and ask for Dr. Robin."

Meghan felt a little hurt. Bell was so short with her, and she sounded so cold. Bell and Meghan had always been somewhat close. Bell even showed her the ropes in dialysis. Why was she acting like this? Today of all days she woke up not feeling well, she was even thinking about calling in to take the day off from work.

"Okay Bell, I'll go. Thanks for calling."

Bell must have heard the hurt in Meghan's voice. She ended with "I'm sorry," and hung up. Sorry about what? *What did Bell know to be sorry about*? After the phone call, Meghan could not stop thinking about why she had to go see a Dr. Robin. She was at her wits end wondering.

Meghan puts on her uniform. She had to go to Mechanize Hospital later anyway. Meghan only did part time with Numerical Dialysis, but the pay and benefits were very good. She took extra care with her hair and make-up that morning.

Granny always said, "When you don't feel good put on your best and make up your face, it will brighten your day."

When Meghan got to the doctor's office, she gave her name to the receptionist. The woman looked like she had seen a ghost. Meghan wondered, *what was the matter. What was going on here*?

"Just a minute, Miss." She knocked a book off the desk, running in the back to get the doctor. She was back within seconds. "This way Mrs. Kramer."

Dr. Robin was a very handsome young man. He stared at Meghan as if she had something on her nose. Meghan started rubbing her face. She was beginning to feel very awkward by now.

Dr. Robin came from behind his desk. "Mrs. Kramer, I'm Dr. Robin. I was expecting some..." He never finished the statement. "I will get right to the point. Mrs. Kramer, your HIV test came back positive." He stopped, for her to say something, but Meghan was just standing there looking at him, not sure if she heard him right feeling afraid.

He repeated it and asked, "Did you hear me?" Meghan eased in the seat he had offered her earlier.

"Mrs. Kramer?"

"Yes."

"I said your test came back positive."

"Doctor that can't be true, I am not a whore, and I have never used drugs in my life. My *ex-husband* never used drugs. My friend does not use drugs, and neither one of them are white nor gay."

Meghan was only speaking from what she knew about HIV. All she knew was gay white men, drug addicts, and streetwalkers were infected with it.

Dr. Robin looked like he was afraid to leave her side. "Can I get you something?"

"No, thank you. Doctor, are you sure you got the right person? I mean, there are a lot of people whose last name is Kramer in this city."

"Mrs. Kramer, I know. Did you do all the tests? Even the western blot also?"

"Yes, we did them all. Dr. Robin, there has to be some mix-up. I want another test.

"You have that right?"

Meghan was getting short of breath; and started hyperventilating. She had to get out of there and fast.

She ran out of his office without looking back. She just could not go to work. She had to get another opinion. Meghan called the job to say she would not be in, without giving anyone an explanation for her absence. She drove to the far south side to a free clinic and got tested again. As she sat waiting to be called, fear took over her mind. She felt it throughout her entire body. This would be another two weeks of torture.

The test just had to be wrong! "How can I tell my children?"

Meghan left, while feeling weak in her legs as if she were going to collapse any minute. Perspiration starts coming out of her pores. Walking on unsteady legs. She got into her car, turned the air conditioner on high positioning the vents directly toward her, and headed home to an empty house, knowing it would take two weeks for the test to come back. She would not tell Tyler, nor would she sleep with him for the next two weeks.

Meghan got home, took a bath, and called her job again. She told them she was sick and needed a few days off. She tried to get a little sleep before her children came home. Also, she had a date with Tyler, which she did not want to keep. Nor did she want the kids to see her in this condition. With what little will power was left in her body, she cooked dinner for the children. Then she slowly dressed for her date with Tyler, wishing she could just lie down and forget this awful mess she was in.

One look at her, and Tyler could tell something was not right. It showed all over her face, and there was no hiding this turmoil she felt. Tyler tries to make small talk as they drove to the restaurant, but her eyes were looking in the opposite direction while her mind was someplace else. Not being one to assume, Tyler just waited, but when he tried to hold her hand while his other hand was steering the wheel of the car, she just moved it out of the way.

"Meghan, all I want to know is if you still love me. I am not a mind reader, but I know when something is wrong with you. Maybe if we talked about whatever it is, we could solve the problem together."

"What makes you think it's a problem we can solve?"

By this time, she had tears in her eyes. Yes! She loved him. If only she could tell him. Not being able to tell him was killing her!

"Ty, I really don't want to talk about it right now. Let's just give it a rest."

She did not want to tell him anything until the next test came back. "Honey, I am not good company tonight, can we just go?"

"Do you want to go someplace else?"

"No!" she said it much too fast. "I would just like to go home." They drive to Meghan's house from the restaurant in silence.

"Okay, will I see you tomorrow?" Meghan just smiles not wanting to give Tyler a reason to ask any more questions that she was not ready to answer, so she said "Maybe," and that was all she could say.

At the door he tried to kiss her, but Meghan pulls away and went inside, and closed the door.

Tyler must have stood there for one or two minutes before he turns and walks away. Meghan had noticed the hurt in Tyler's eyes, when she looked through the window, but what could she say?

Tyler went and got himself a drink, a bottle of Crown that had been in the car for over three weeks. In the old days, he would have drunk it in one day. He felt he really needed a drink over this situation.

Tyler's first thought was to find Linda and ask what was wrong, but he took a second thought and decided against it. Instead, he goes home and tries to sleep. For the first time, he knew real hurt, and the pain of rejection from Meghan. It almost felt as worse as how his wife made him feel when he found out she was having an affair.

The next morning Tyler calls her, but was told she left early for work. Mark answered. Tyler just had to ask Mark if Meghan seemed upset.

"No, I really didn't get a good look at her I couldn't tell. Is there something wrong, sir?"

"No, I was just a little worried about her. She did not seem to be feeling very well last night." Tyler didn't want the children to become alarmed about her.

In addition, of all days Betty got up this morning wanting to talk to him. Tyler had heard through the grapevine that her lover was very sick a few weeks earlier. Tyler was sure something had happened to him, or why else would she want to talk to him? Betty could have just written a note and left it on his car like she always did. Tyler told her he would get back to her and left to use the phone in private. Tyler had to speak to Meghan.

She returns to work after taking a few days off. This would not be a good day at work. With the same answer, "She is with a patient," Tyler knew not to try again.

THE LONGEST DAY

Meghan decided to work a double shift that day. But when she arrived home, Tyler was at her house waiting in his car. This time she would not be able to dodge him.

"Meghan we really need to talk. If there is something I have done, you can tell me. Don't just cut me off like this."

"Tyler, if I ask you to do something for me, would you?"

"You know I will do anything for you, because I love you."

"Will you give me two more weeks alone? I had some tests done and it will take two weeks for the results to come back. Can you give me that?"

Tyler did not want to go back on his word, so he agreed to it. Tyler wants to ask what kind of tests; however, he decides to wait. She would tell him if she wanted him to know. That was one of the reasons they had hit it off so well. They both knew when to give the other one space.

Meghan's heart was breaking, but she could not tell Tyler what the doctor told her. Tyler walked away with his head down, something Meghan had never seen him do before. It only made her feel worse. Tyler was a man that always held his head up high.

The next two weeks Meghan was working like a dog. By this time, the children and Linda had noticed a change, but no one in the bunch had the nerves to really say anything. Besides, Meghan looked like a mental patient! Everyone just stayed out of her way. She stopped wearing make-up. Until now she had always taken pride in her looks, but it was as if she did not care. She would get up early and take a shower, and get out of the house before the kids were out of bed. Her boss had warned her that if she didn't stop clocking in so early, she would have to be written up. Meghan was upset about that too.

"The Bitch is going to write me up for coming in too early, and the rest of the staff were always coming in late."

Meghan could not understand why they were never happy. She had set up everything by the time they got there! What was the problem?

This really made Meghan feel like the world was against her. What kind of God would put her in this fix! Meghan knew it was time to talk to someone or she was going to lose her mind. The first person that crossed her mind was her pastor, at that time Reverend Hawkins. Meghan could always talk to him, and it would stay between them. Sunday could not come fast enough for her.

SUNDAY MORNING CONFESSION

That Sunday Meghan was the first one at church, but the pastor was busy. So, this meant she had to wait. Meghan was going to make sure she was the first one in Pastor's office after church. It took her all of five minutes to tell Reverend Hawkins the entire story. Meghan was a mess.

Pastor Hawkins just put his arms around her. "It's going to be okay, sister Kramer!" Meghan wishes she could pull from his faith because hers was fading fast. She thought to herself, *how could God let this happen to me*? She tried to live right, be a good Christian, get married, and play by the rules. Now this! She wants to die. She could not take it if people discriminated against her the way some of the doctors, nurses or techs treats their patients with HIV/Aids.

This was going to be a very long two weeks, waiting for the results of another HIV test. She feels so much stress, and the wait seems unbearable. *God, why does it take so long for the results to come back*? Meghan wants to cry more, but her eyes would give her away around the kids, and Mark was watching her like a hawk. Every time Meghan walked in, Mark would meet her at the door, with that look on his face, "What's wrong?"

JUST NO LYING TO MARK

The day of the second test results Meghan broke down. The tears would not stop. She worked a double shift, trying not to think about what the nurse had said. But on the way home it hit her, as she was driving, the scene kept running through her mind. It seemed as if it took the nurse three minutes to make six steps. Meghan's heart was beating so fast that she was getting SOB (shortness of breath) from the wait. Her head hurt, her hands were sweaty, and she could feel the tears building up in her eyes, just by the look on the nurse's face.

"Ms. I am so sorry, but the test results were positive." Why were they doing this to her? She was sure they had the wrong person. There was no doubt in her mind! After the talk with her pastor, there had been a little hope in the back of her mind that they were wrong. But now it seems to be more real, especially after two positive results. It had to be a mistake. None of the stigma fit her. "Is there anyone you would like me to call?" The nurse's voice got Meghan's attention again. She continued to speak, asking Meghan if she was all right. After collecting her thoughts, Meghan realized where she was and what was going on.

"No, there is no one to call. I'll be all right. Thank you."

As she walks out of the clinic her legs just wants to stop. "God, if I wasn't afraid of hell, I would kill myself; just drive my car into Lake Michigan or into a wall."

All the things Meghan had heard about HIV came to mind again: only drug addicts, prostitutes, gay white men, liberal young black men, and some homeless people contracted HIV/Aids. Why hadn't it been learned that everyone is at risk if you have sex. If so, then Meghan may not have had quite the same reaction from her test results. Here Meghan was, just the opposite: tall, lovely, with a fine home, good job, most of all great children.

"Oh, my God!" By the grace of God Meghan made it home and got into bed. But rest was out of the question. There was no rest for this weary soul.

Meghan was up, and in the kitchen when Mark came in. Mark was the first one home. Any other time Mark would have stayed at school playing ball, but he was worried about Meghan.

"Mom, now that we are alone, would you please tell me what's wrong?"

As Meghan looked into his young eyes, she knew she had to tell the truth. That was the pact Meghan made with him a very long time ago. If Mark were man enough to ask, Meghan would be woman enough to tell him the truth, no matter what it was.

"Mark, sit down." The tears started again.

"I just came from the clinic for the second test, and they said I am HIV positive."

This was the second time Meghan said the acronym. Mark's face did not change, but his eyes had so much sorrow in them.

"Is that why when Magic Johnson was on TV, two weeks ago, you asked what I would do if you told me that?"

"Yes!" She had forgotten about the incident since she was so upset. For about ten minutes, neither said anything until Meghan got some control.

"Mom, is that what's been wrong for the past month?"

"Yes."

"Have you talked to Mr. Scottsdale about this?"

"No. I wouldn't know where to start."

"Just tell him what the doctor and the clinic staff told you." Mark was trying to fight back the tears also.

"I will. I must get another test. I just can't believe them. I never used drugs. You know I'm not a gay white man."

This was all Meghan could think of. But Meghan could swear there was something else in Mark's eyes, she just was not sure what it was.

At that point, Mark wanted to tell his mother some of the things he had heard about Nick, but Mark decided against it. "When are you going to get another test?"

"Tomorrow, I will go to another place where no one knows me."

Mark just sat there holding his mother's hands. After what seemed like hours, he heard Nicole, Rachel, and Tina come in.

"Mark, I don't want them to see me like this!" Meghan returned to her room.

"Okay, just get some rest. I will tell them you're not feeling well."

"Thanks baby." Mark left Meghan and went to greet his sisters.

"Where is mom?" Rachel asked.

"She isn't feeling well, fix your own dinner." Mark knew he did not want anything to eat. The thought of his mother dying was just too much to cope with right now. Mark went to his room and cried.

Nicole, Tina, and Rachel got something to eat. There was always something nutritious left over from the previous meal. After eating, and doing the dishes they sat at the kitchen table to do their homework. By that time, Linda comes home.

"Where is your mom? and Mark?"

"Mom is not feeling well. She's in her room. Mark is in his room doing homework or just reading," Rachel said.

Linda thought to knock on Meghan's door but changes her mind. She decided to let her rest.

Meghan seems to have a lot on her mind. Whatever it is, it had Tyler upset also.

Linda decides to take a bath and soak her busy day off her so that she could go out. She feels revived. To her surprise, Tyler was having a few drinks with Red.

Linda says, "You mean you are hanging with the little people again."

Linda looks confused. "What's wrong with you and Meghan? I'm not used to seeing you without her."

"Well get used to it. I'm trying hard to get used to it. Meghan told me she needed some time for herself."

"Well, if it's any consolation, Meghan is home in bed not feeling well."

"Is she sick?"

"No, I don't think so. I didn't see her. The girls just said she wanted to rest."

"I will try to call her again."

"Good luck." Linda said.

Tyler dialed the number. Mark answered the phone.

"Hi Mark"

"Hi Mr. Scottsdale."

"Son, is your mother home?"

"Yes sir, but she told us she didn't want to talk to anyone."

"I guess that means me also."

"Yes sir, but I will tell her you called."

A strange silence followed. After a moment, Mark spoke again. "Mr. Scottsdale, mom really cares about you. I hope you know that."

"Thank you, Mark. I know she does. And I care about her tremendously." Good night, son."

"Good night, Mr. Scottsdale."

They hung up. Mark felt he just had to say that. He could hear the disappointment in Tyler's voice. Mark wondered *how Tyler was going to treat his mom when she told him about the tests results.* Mark knew what the kids at school would say, but this was his MOM. She was different, unlike the rest. Besides, he would kill someone if they said something wrong about his mother.

NO LUCK!!!

Tyler went back to where Red and Linda were.

Linda spoke first, "No luck?"

"No, Mark answered the phone."

"Tyler I am not sure, but I know Meghan has been to the doctor twice in the past month. It started around the first week of last month. ·I want to talk to her, but I know she will tell me when she wants me to know." They all ordered another drink and changed the subject.

Tyler left and drove by Meghan's house. No light was on in her bedroom and her car was there. Tyler wanted to try to phone again but drove home instead. To make matters worse, Betty was home. He parked the car and went into the basement. That way Betty would leave him alone.

For the first time in twenty years, Tyler felt like crying. The last time Tyler felt like this was when his mother died. If he only had someone to talk to. He got a drink, put some blues on, and sat back thinking about this whole thing, *the situation that was happening.* By the time Tyler got upstairs

Betty was asleep in her room, and it was too late to call Meghan. He just went to his room and went to bed.

The next morning Linda was up at 6:00 a.m. She found that Meghan had already left. Linda called Meghan's job. She just wanted to hear her sister's voice. When Meghan's name was called for the phone, her heart stopped. Thinking it might be one of the kids Meghan went and answered the phone.

"Meghan, girl, what is going on with you?" "Are you mad at me, Meg?" "Do you want to talk about it?"

"Lyn, I can't talk about this right now." They both, only used half of each other's names, when they were having sister talks.

"Meg, Tyler is about to lose his mind."

"I know Lyn, but I can't talk to him yet."

"It's that bad, Meg?" Linda asked.

"Lyn, I will be okay. I have to...."

But she could not tell Linda. Linda would act hard, but Meghan knew under that shell Linda was all heart when it comes to her. So, this was something she would have to carry alone.

Every time Meghan had a feeling that she wanted to die she would call Pastor Hawkins. He would pray with her. Meghan always told him the truth even about Tyler and the way she started drinking again. Even Meghan was worried because that was a secret life she did not want to return to. Even Linda did not know that Meghan was a border line alcoholic at one time. This all happened when she was living away and traveling all the time. As a matter of a fact, that seemed like another lifetime ago. At that time, she was traveling, selling magazines door-to-door, drinking, and other things Meghan refused to think about at this time.

Linda tried again to get her to talk. "Are you pregnant?"

"Girl you know better than that. I wish I were, that would be better than...." She just stopped talking.

Linda knew that whatever it was, it was bad!

Meghan went back to thinking about how it was back then. *On the edge between the stress of everyday life, her job, and the loneliness she felt, anyone would have turned to drinking.* Then once she left the crew, she learned that she had cancer. But she fought with her doctor's help, and it went into remission. Now this! Meghan's mind was running a mile a minute. She starts thinking about the children's father and *how he did not want to have anything to do with her when she got pregnant with Tina, saying he could not afford all these babies.* He talked like she could. However, even with that she pulled herself up and went back to school and made it. That's where she met Nick. Linda's voice brought her back to reality.

"Meg, where are you? You stopped talking."

"Look Lyn, I will talk to you when I get home." Knowing she would not talk to Linda about this, Meghan would have to make up something else, but not this!

"Okay girl, I will let you go. See you tonight."

Going back to work, Meghan was still thinking about *Wade, and the way he rejected her.* She never told her family the real story. Meghan never told them how Wade had tried to kill her in her sleep. That was when Meghan knew she had to get away from him. Mark was young and the girls were small. She was pregnant with Tina at that time about six weeks, and Meghan would never let her children grow up in a house like that. At that time, she was six weeks pregnant. Wade said too many babies would mess up her body. He made it plain he was in love with her looks, not so much with her.

The fact is he made it very plain. He would put up with three kids, but not another one, like she screwed herself.

When they met Wade was so nice and sweet, wining and dining her. In a way, Wade and Nick were a lot alike. They were both very handsome men, and maybe she should have said boys like her family called them.

After a while, Wade became mean and strict. She could never even look at another man. However, that cold night when she left with her children with the clothes on their backs, Meghan had, had enough.

The women's shelter helped her forget her hurt and they relocated her. She moved on after that, and did not look back. The judge said Wade could see the kids, but he could not come near Meghan. So, she just said Wade could see them when they wanted to see him. Shortly after that, Wade went to jail for trying to kill his girlfriend and her family. Meghan had no worries about him finding her.

"Mrs. Kramer, Mrs. Kramer." A patient was calling her; one of her machines had stopped. Getting back to work took her mind off things.

Later that evening on the way home from work, Meghan decides to call Linda and tell her about her day at work and maybe she would forget about the rest. It was a very hard day. When Meghan got home, things were quiet.

Linda was out, and the children were doing their own thing. So, she had a little time for herself. Meghan really wanted to call Tyler, but changed her mind. Instead, she went and took a long bubble bath, giving herself some time to think.

Why was she thinking about Wade today? The man had been out her life for years, now he was occupying her thoughts. In his own way, she thinks he really loved her, but he sure had a hell of a way of showing it. Her mind thinks back again, *the man had tried to kill her while she was sleeping*. That's when she knew it was time to get out of there.

About several years later Meghan met Nick in college. Meghan had gone back after the big strike with Cage. She was going for nursing and Nick was going to become a renal technologist.

Nick had a smile that would light up the world. They had a lot in common. Both from the South, both had a dislike for their fathers, and could not see why their mothers stayed with them.

People did not see Nick as Meghan saw him. Meghan's Granny did not like Nick at all. But some women were always in his face, even her friends. The man really had sex appeal, and he knew it. Even men liked him. Nick was always respected on the job, and everywhere else he went.

AFTER TWO MORE WEEKS OF HELL

Today was the last day after two more weeks of pure hell. Meghan was going back for the third test. She was sure this one would be different. It just had to be. There was no way she could be HIV positive. There had to be a mistake or a mix up in the names. Meghan walked through the doors, dressed in her nurse uniform (as if that would make a difference). She approached the young lady at the desk and gave her the slip of paper with a number on it. The lady took it saying nothing, but giving her a look like "not you too." Meghan stood and waited, mouth dry, palms wet, and legs shaking. She was a mess trying to keep it together.

A middle-aged woman walked over to her with that damn look in her eyes, the same one that she had seen twice before. Meghan wanted to turn and run, but her legs were not sturdy enough and she was afraid of falling, so she just stood as the woman came to escort her to a private room.

"Hi, I am Dr. Glen. I know this is hard for you, but I'm sorry. Your test was positive."

Meghan just stood there looking at her.

The doctor spoke again, "Can I get you something?"

"No, I'm okay."

"Are you driving?"

"Yes!" She said it with a dry voice; it did not sound like hers.

"You can sit, and we can talk if you have time." Dr. Glen stated.

"No, thank you. I have to get out of here!"

"How do I tell my partner?" she asked.

"He might have infected you."

"No, I doubt that."

Meghan was trying so hard to keep her face from telling her story to others that were sitting in the waiting area as she was leaving. She knew they did not hear what the doctor had said, but even a fool could tell it was not good news.

Meghan left without taking the paper. Instead, she pages Tyler, Tyler calls her right back as if he were expecting her to reach out to him sooner than later.

"I need you to meet me at Stony and Ninety-fifth. You will see my car.

"Meghan is everything alright?"

"Just meet me there, please." Meghan was almost screaming by this time.

"Okay! Okay! I'll be there." Meghan knew he had to get to work. But she thought to herself that *he might not want to go to work after hearing what she has to say*.

It only took her ten minutes to get there. Tyler was already there. The look on Meghan's face said, please do not touch me. So, Tyler stood back.

"Tyler, I will make this fast."

Quickly she said, "I have HIV. I was diagnosed recently and took three tests hoping one would come back negative."

Meghan told him the whole story from day one. Meghan could see the life go out his face.

Then Tyler said the words that almost made her HATE him.

"Meghan, I never would have told you this."

"What? Are you out your damn mind? You wouldn't have told me?"

"No! I would've just kept doing what we were doing."

"Well Tyler I couldn't; I had to tell you. I would never keep this from someone."

Meghan felt like Tyler had kicked her in the stomach. Not knowing what else to say she just lost it. Eight weeks of tears started rolling down her face.

"How can you say you wouldn't have told me?"

"Meghan please, I didn't say that to hurt you. I just meant I don't care. I still want to be with you."

"No! No! Hell no! How can you want to touch me? I'm dirty ... I am going to die! I might have infected you." At that point, she stopped crying as Tyler wipes her tears with his handkerchief.

"Look, I'm going right now and get tested."

"Okay." This makes me feel better. Your results will be back in two weeks."

"Do you still love me?"

"Yes, I just need the two weeks that it is going to take your test results to come back. Will you give me some time?"

Meghan only took five minutes of Tyler's time, and he was off to work. Meghan drove to the place where she found serenity. She was still distraught and could not go to work. She spent enough time at the lake, thinking about *her and Tyler's relationship*. Meghan was heartbroken and flustered, so she decided to go home.

She was home in 20 minutes. As she was sticking the key in the keyhole, the phone was ringing. She rushes to answer it with haste in her voice, only to be disappointed when she heard Perry's voice.

"Hi Meghan, this is Perry."

"Perry!" Perry was Nick's roommate. What did Perry want with her? They had not talked very much.

"Yes, Perry. What can I do for you?" Meghan asked.

"I was hoping we could talk."

"About what?"

"Meghan, I really need to talk to you. How did the girls like their dresses?"

"Perry, I don't want to be rude, but I just came from the doctor for the third time with some very bad news."

"What did the doctors say?"

"That's none of your business. Why are you calling me anyway?"

"I just thought we could talk...."

"What!" Meghan felt as if her mind was playing tricks on her.

"Meghan, you can tell me what the doctors said." He was talking to her as if they were best friends.

"Perry, we are not friends."

"Okay Meghan, if you won't tell me, let me tell you." Perry's tone changed. "The doctors said you are HIV positive."

Perry thought she didn't hear him, so he repeated it again. "The doctors said you are HIV positive."

"The reason I know is because I told Nick I was infected when we got involved, but he said it didn't matter."

Meghan could not move. She froze.

"Meghan, you mean, you didn't know Nick is bisexual?"

His voice was a little more than a whisper. "He told me once you did know. Meghan, I didn't call to hurt you. I called to ask you to forgive me for my part in this. Nick said you were a loose woman. He said, you both were sleeping around, and into swinging. I know now that was a lie. I have been watching you for the past two years. I know you've only seen one guy, and that was after you and Nick were separated for almost two years."

My God, this man had been stalking her! Why couldn't she hang up the phone? Perry went on to talk about the preachers, deacons, and celebrities that Nick had been with. Meghan's body was stuck. She was thinking about what she had heard! These were not men you would think of when you heard the word 'gay'. These were macho men, who would beat up a gay guy … and Nick was a gay basher all the way!

"Meghan, Nick did me wrong also. Nick took my money and now he has moved on with someone else."

"Why are you telling me all this?"

"Meghan please don't hate me. Try to forgive me. Nick had another man at your house when you went to Mississippi to see your mother, (that was before her mother died. Meghan had gone to the family reunion) when he got you that new truck," Perry said."

Nick had told this man all their business and the rest he found out on his own.

"I don't want to hurt you, but women like you need to know what they are up against these days…."

"Goodbye Perry!" Finally, her hand was able to take a command from her brain.

SHE HAD TO TALK TO NICK

Slamming the phone down with such force, thinking it was broken, Meghan's head was spinning. Her mouth was so dry. She had to calm down. Not wanting her voice to give her away, Meghan dialed Nick Kramer's number. Nick answered with that all-too-familiar, care-free I don't give-a-damn voice. Meghan wanted to kill him, but the thought of jail was not good, and killing herself meant hell. She thought, *Why was this happening to me*? Meghan had always prayed, and tried to do well by others. Not saying she was perfect, but she tried to be a good person.

"Nick, I got a call from Perry!" She went on to tell him everything that was said. Nick just listened not saying anything until she stopped talking. Meghan did not take a breath between words.

"Meghan, Perry is lying, and you're crazy! I'm not going to listen to this shit! Goodbye."

He hung up. Not even so much as a how are you doing? In her mind, Meghan pictured him saying those words to her face.

Meghan was at a loss for words. This man had put her life in danger just because he could not keep his rod in his pants. She knew Nick was sleeping with other women, but now this.... It was rumored that Nick was sleeping with women on his job. She guessed men also! Only God knew what this said about her.

Before Meghan changed clothes, she got up, totally undressed, and just stood in front of the mirror. She was a nice-looking woman. But all of a sudden, she felt ugly. She dressed in a hurry, and just sat and cried until there were no more tears.

Tyler calls. "Meghan, please don't be mad at me for what I said earlier. I just meant I'm not going to lose my life and you, too!"

"Tyler we will talk when your test comes back."

Meghan did not feel like telling him about the calls with Perry or Nick. All the while, she was praying he was not positive.

The next two weeks everyone could tell she was a ticking time bomb. Meghan walked around for three days in the same clothes with her head down. She is not her usual self. Every time she reaches for something in the kitchen cabinets, she slams the cabinet doors. Normally, she picks up her feet while walking. Now, she drags and scraps her feet across the wooden floor sounding like sandpaper. She has not showered either. You can smell a stitch like yellow onions fumigating from her bedroom.

They stayed out of her way. Linda did not try to talk to her. Linda sitting at the breakfast nook in the kitchen drinking her morning tea when Meghan enters the kitchen. Linda looks up from reading a book of her favorite author Mary Higgins Clark, an America mystery suspense writer. The expression on Meghan's face expressed sadness. The inner corners of her eyebrows drawn up, The corners of her mouth drawn down, and her eyes intensely staring with anger.

Meghan says something snappy to Linda and from that point, Linda knew not to say anything.

Only the kids would come near her, and Mark was the only one who really knew. He understood.

Nicole said once, "Mom's a real BITCH."

Mark jumps all over her. "Mom is under a lot of pressure. You should keep your mouth shut!"

Nicole and Rachel just looked at each other. Tina did not say anything, knowing whatever it was Mark knew. But he was not about to tell them, and they had better not ask. At that point they could tell Mark was upset about it also.

After a while, Meghan realizes that being upset and angry was not going to change anything. In fact, it was making her sicker. Her body starts showing signs that something was not right. She feels weak but could not sleep because of the thought of Tyler's test results. She paces her bedroom floor worrying.

THE END OF THE TWO WEEKS - TYLER'S TEST

The night before Tyler would receive his test results, he calls Meghan. She looks at her phone ringing hesitant to answer. She then grabs the receiver quickly right before the call goes into voice mail and says, "Hello," with worry in her voice.

"Hi Meghan. I was calling to see if you would be going to the doctor's office with me."

"If you want me to. I am feeling a little low."

"Let me come and see you."

"No, it won't help."

"I believe it will."

"Let's just wait and see one another tomorrow. I will get myself together. It has not been good."

The day Tyler went for his test results, Meghan could not eat. Nor did she sleep the night before. In spite of not eating and exhausted from not sleeping, she was able to go with him. As the nurse came across the room, she did not have *the look on her face*, as Meghan called it. Especially not the look the nurses had when they were about to give results to her. The nurse smiles slightly.

"We got the results."

"You can tell both of us."

"Well, Sir, your test came back negative."

Meghan just started crying and thanking God. "But, if you have had sex in the past month, you will need to be tested again," the nurse added.

"Well, I will not have to be tested again!" Tyler stated, looking at Meghan. If she had to guess, he looked downright disappointed.

Meghan spoke first, "Tyler I am so happy for you." Then she told him about the phone call from Perry, and how Nick had responded to her call. Tyler did not say anything, but they both knew that if he saw Nick anytime soon Tyler would kick his ass from A-Z. How could Nick have done this to a woman like her?

"Meghan, can we get back to normal now?"

"Ty, I'm not sure I can."

This was not the answer Tyler was expecting, that's why (in a way) he wanted his test to return positive also, and then they would have more of a chance to stay together.

"Ty, I feel my life is over. I don't know much about this illness except I'm going to die soon."

"How can you say that?" Tyler was wondering why Meghan was giving up. This was a woman that would not let her children use the words 'if' and 'can't' or anything that leads to failure. Tyler knew it would take time, and that Meghan would come back into her own.

The thought of being sexually active with someone knowing she has HIV is devasting. Meghan does not have all the facts about it. She feels nasty, violated, and leery about dealing with anyone. The thought of *Tyler being in the incubation stage and that maybe he will test positive one day* keeps going over and over in her mind.

"Meghan, I have been doing a lot of reading about HIV, and people are living much longer now. You just have to take care of yourself. But that did not change her mind about dating Tyler anymore.

Meghan made an appointment with an HIV doctor to find out if there is a cure for this disease in the works. When Meghan walked into the office, she looked around, wanting to run. Every woman Meghan saw were drug addicts, prostitutes, or homeless people just looking lost. At first, some took Meghan for a doctor or group leader, not a client. When they found out she was infected, some people were mean to her, even downright hateful.

The nurse came out and calls Ms. Kramer. Meghan stood and started walking toward the doctor's office. The nurse took her vitals and asks several questions about how Meghan is feeling. The doctor comes into exam Meghan. When the examination was over, the doctor shares information to help Meghan on what to do and medicines to take.

The doctor's approach was very nice, but she told Meghan the truth that she had only about five years to live. This gave Meghan very little hope.

"Five years? I want to live to see my children grow up." She was looking for any kind of hope in the doctor's eyes, but saw none. Only pity!

After returning home, Meghan went to bed without saying anything to anyone. Calling Tyler was out the question! What could she say to him, that she was going to die in five years?

TIME PASSED

As time went by, Meghan was pushing Tyler away. She even encourages him to find someone else. Every time she saw him Tyler's eyes looked as if he had been weeping, there was a hurt in his eyes that stuck in Meghan's mind. It just broke her heart to see him that way. She was telling him one thing because she loved him. At the same time, she was feeling something else because she cares for him. She really loved him, and she knew his love for her was just as genuine as she felt about him.

Work was a nightmare. Meghan was so afraid someone would know her secret. Meghan was thinking repeatedly in her mind, *this is a lot of pressure having to come in to work with the thought of my secret of being infected with HIV spreading through the hospital and people treating me differently, is a nightmare.*

Each time she went to the doctor she would be on her way to work, in her uniform. That way she expected the doctors and the nurses to treat her differently.

PREJUDICE and OTHER LESSONS

One day Meghan went into the office wearing her street clothes. One of the interns refused to draw her blood when he saw the word HIV on her chart. Meghan told Dr. Jones what had happened.

The doctor went to the lab and went off! She asked for the charge nurse and told her, "I want that person out of here. This is not the place for prejudice!" Meghan was sad the person lost their job, although, she took care of people every day that she preferred not to care for. In this career, you cannot pick and choose who you will serve.

Meghan could not show her real feelings on the job. She was a nurse and had taken an oath to help people. She was not to judge them or their lifestyle, creed, or character. So, in this particular case, the young man got what he deserved, based on his behavior. Another time a young lady was about to draw Meghan's blood without gloves. Meghan stopped the girl, and asked why she was not wearing protective gloves.

"You are a special case," the young lady stated. "You're not a drug addict or streetwalker."

"No, but I'm HIV positive. It doesn't matter how I got it. I'm still going to die from AIDS unless something changes," Meghan replied.

The nurse looked at Meghan as if she had slapped her in the face. Meghan was really mad by this time. She was beginning to understand something firsthand. It was just how prejudiced and naïve some of the medical staff were towards HIV/Aids patients. One day Meghan overheard Joe, one of the techs, say "Why are we wasting time and medication on them. They are going to die anyway?" This was in the early '90s. Meghan was thinking to herself, *IT'S NOT OVER TILL GOD SAYS IT'S OVER*!

Finally, after a few months there, Meghan stopped going to Dr. Jones's clinic with the group. She just went to her medical doctor, Dr. Edward. She had stated once that she knew nothing about HIV, but they would learn together. Dr. Edward had gotten Meghan to take another test for her records. Meghan did, all the time hoping it would be different, but knowing it would be the same.

LIFE GOES ON!

After a while, Meghan did begin to cope better. Oh! She thought but then she noticed she was drinking more and more. By this time, she had begun to let Tyler come back around. He would buy the alcohol for her. Tyler knew it was wrong, but he wanted to be with Meghan anyway he could. When she was drinking, she was lively, friendly, and very warm towards him. He thought, *How long could this last?* Tyler knew Meghan was not the kind of woman that would live like this for long, but he would enjoy it while he could.

*   *   *

Time had gone by Tyler and Meghan hadn't seen one another in a while. As a matter of fact, one day, they decide to go fishing and Tyler was the one that was not able to keep his hands off Meghan. They were in the car and this time he was all over her in the front seat and when Meghan looks up, she could see the lake security who was parked watching them as if he were watching a movie.

The security guard decides to walk closer to the car to see what is actually happening. When Meghan opens her eyes and looks up, her eyes were looking directly in the security guard's eyes. She tried pushing Tyler's head up and he looked up and asked, "Do you know him?"

"No."

"Don't bother me."

And Tyler continues helping Meghan feel like a woman.

Meghan looks at the security guard and smirks.

He walks away after smiling.

Back at home, the children noticed Meghan was not always on them. In other words, she did not complain about anything they were doing. Little did they know she was drinking!

Some days Meghan would be drinking before work. There was this one patient, David that seemed to always know. He would say something like, "Ms. Kramer you must've had a good weekend." David came twice a week, Monday's, and Friday's. If it were Friday, he would say, "Thursday was good." Meghan would just smile.

Meghan notices something else. It seems men found her more attractive. Or maybe it was because she did not want to be bothered with any of them. She even stopped wearing make-up, and she is downright mean to Tyler. But he still wants to be around her. She just wants him to drink with her, and take her out. For some unapparent reason she just didn't want to drink alone! This went on for months. Then one night, after having too much to drink, nearly drunk, she said, "My God, what do I have to do to get rid of you?"

"You will never get rid of me."

Meghan knew her life was spinning out of control, and there was nothing she could do about it. Tyler was drinking just as much as she was.

One morning Christina, her boss, calls Meghan into the office to talk about her drinking, and her status. Two weeks later, Meghan comes to work and Christina asks her to come to her office. As Meghan was walking toward Christina's office, she feels a gut-wrenching feeling that this is probably it for me here.

A few days after the meeting Meghan overheard Christina on the phone talking to someone, "I can't have an infected nurse working with my patients. It's bad enough we have infected patients, now a nurse, and she is drinking as well!" This was a wakeup call, in a way, for Meghan.

Christina says, "Meghan have a seat."

Meghan thought, *good morning to you too*.

"Meghan, we have noticed that you are still drinking, and the patients think you are drinking on the job."

Meghan continues to listen.

You have been a star nurse here and we want you to get some help. We have to let you go and here is a pamphlet to a great place that can provide you the help you need. Take this time off to regroup and find yourself.

Meghan leaves out of Christina's office quietly and gathers her personal items and left without talking to anyone.

NEW JOB

Getting another job was not a problem. Nurses were in demand, but Meghan did take four weeks off before taking full time with Numerical. They were glad to get her back. They knew she was a very hard worker because she had worked for them part time a few years ago. Even Bell was happy to have Meghan full time. She was warmer toward Meghan, but they never talked about her status. She knew Bell knew, but she would never discuss it with her. Bell was very professional with everything and everyone.

Now Meghan had to find a job part time with another facility. She finds a job at Hope Center in the Acute Dialysis Department. She would work mostly on the weekends, hoping this would keep her too busy to think about her condition. Also, this arrangement keeps Tyler and her apart from one another. She thought, *maybe I can just get sober and get my life under control again.*

NOWHERE TO HIDE

There were moments where Meghan thought about starting over. Meghan would think about empty dreams she experienced on the Magazine Crew even the ones Linda did not know about. *Lord, it seems so long ago.* That was three years of expensive education that college could not give. She thought *she must have at least gotten a master's degree in life, if not a doctorate.*

The town, the people she met, all made her grow up very fast. That was before Wade. One of Meghan's friends had talked her into going. They would be selling books. Door-to-door was the good part. The life on Crew was a different story. Thank God she did not get caught up in drugs, but she did drink like a fish. The abortions, the women being passed from man to man! It was enough to make you drink, and to drink a lot. Thank God, she got away when she did.

Meghan had to wonder what would have happened if she had stayed there. One thing, she would not have been HIV positive, but how could you know? She might have even gotten it sooner.

Meghan had to pull herself together, or she would be back in the bottle, like before. That day she called the hot line for AA (Alcohol Anonymous), made an appointment, and started going.

About three days later Meghan calls Tyler, and told him about it. She also told him she was going back to church. It was as if God was telling her something. She wanted to know exactly what it was that He was speaking. All Meghan could think about was Psalm 37:4. *If she would seek God, and then delight herself in His ways, He would give her the desires of her heart.*

In the back of her mind, it was as if she could hear her mother saying, Train up a child in the way he should go, and when he is old, he will not depart from it. (Proverbs 22:6)

That Sunday morning Meghan was at church before anyone else. Mother Davis was so glad to see Meghan. She did not ask anything. They just hugged each other for about five minutes, both of them crying, and thanking God. Meghan felt like the prodigal son in the Bible (ref. Luke 15:11-32). She was finally home!

Meghan was not all flowers and sunshine. She would slip, confess, sleep with Tyler, and feel like dirt the next day. Her relationship with God was too important and she knew she needed God's help only he could help her. About three years of this and Meghan could not take it anymore. She had stopped seeing Tyler altogether.

While she was hugging Mother Davis, her mind traveled back to one night when she slipped. *Tyler came to the door and asked Meghan if they could talk for a moment. He had already rented a room and wanted her to go and talk with him. She knew that they were going to be doing more than talking. Meghan really needed to be with Tyler. She missed him and the great times they had. When they got to the room, he made it seem as if they were going to be talking. As soon as he opened the door, she saw rose peddles, a banquet of long stem red roses, candles burning, a bottle of champaign on ice, and she could smell the aroma of oil smelling like the cologne that he wears which melted her heart. It was an erotic scent. At that moment, Meghan had forgot all about the pain, the suffering, the illness, everything left out of her mind. She could not resist. It was tantalizing. He hadn't touched her, and she could still feel his hands all over her body. When Meghan turned around all she could see was COME HERE BABY AND LET ME ROCK YOUR WORLD. Tyler did not have to say a word. The scene was setup for love making, and she was all his. He could do whatever he wanted to do with her.*

He picked her up and laid her on the bed. She was very submissive to him. He undressed her from the waist down. He took his tongue and started licking Meghan's inner thighs. At that point, her body was out of her control. All she could do was open wide.

After that Meghan confessed to God and repented for forgetting that she was still HIV positive.

Tyler knew that he did not make it easy for Meghan to resist. He was hurt, but said, "My arms are too short to box with God."

On June 12, 1995, they just kissed and said goodbye.

Meghan's life becomes a new trend, home, work, and church. Even the children were going to church with her. Mark was just glad to see his mother smile again – and not drunk! He knew Meghan had a drinking problem. He watched her behavior change when she drank and would wisely talk with her about what was best for her. He was wise beyond his years.

Mark felt this is a great time to go away to college. He got accepted at Northern Illinois and Ohio State. He decided on Ohio State. Little did

Meghan know, Tyler helped Mark with his applications.

YEARS PASSED

Meghan enjoyed taking trips with the church. The pastor always wanted her to drive. He noticed that she is a safe driver.

In September 1995 the Labor Day weekend, the church was going to Toledo, Ohio. Meghan was not excited about going. Later at the conference she found out Juanita Bynum was there. She is a well renowned speaker known for her "No More Sheets" message. During that time, Meghan had lots of hate in her heart from how Nick treated her when they were together and even after they separated.

At the conference in one of the sessions, Meghan was standing with others in attendance. Toward the end of the service, Juanita Bynum and Bishop James walked directly toward where Meghan was standing. Meghan thought she was going to someone else. Juanita Bynum laid hands on Meghan's head and said sternly, "LET-GO-AND-LET-GOD!" It was as if she could feel the hate leaving her body immediately. Meghan went to another place in God.

It was after the trip to Toledo, Ohio that Meghan came home feeling very good after meeting Juanita Bynum. The subject had been on forgiveness. She had meditated on it all week. Meghan had made it back home and that Friday night the real test came.

Meghan and Tina had just come from Bible study. They seemed to spend more time together. Mark was away in collage. Nicole and Rachel were out with friends. Linda was out also.

When Meghan pulled up, Nick was standing on the side of his car. Tina said, "Mom, he looks crazy! Maybe we shouldn't stop at home."

"It's okay baby."

Meghan assured Tina. She got out first. Nick had half a smile on his face. They hadn't talked in three weeks. Each time they had talked, he seemed to have a problem. Meghan just wanted to know what he wanted now.

"Meghan, I didn't know where else to go. I just got back from Georgia only to find I had been robbed. They took everything in my place, even broke my fish tank."

Meghan knew he loved that tank. She did not have anything to say. She could not think of anything. She just stood there looking at him.

Nick looked so lost, and all of sudden another Bible verse came to her mind. God will make your enemies your footstool. (ref. Hebrew 1:13.) God knows, over the years Nick had been very mean toward her in several different ways.

"Mark's room is empty. You can use it."

Meghan did not see Nick as the man who had caused her so much hurt and pain. She did not see him as the man who had possibly acted in a way to cause her to lose her life early. All she could see was a person that needed her help. She saw him as a stranger, among those to whom Jesus desires that we minister.

Tina looked at her mother as if she had lost her mind, but did not say a word. Meghan and Tina helped him get his stuff into the attic. Afterwards, Meghan asked Nick if he was hungry. Nick said that he was, but he did not want to put a strain on Meghan.

She made him a sandwich, gave him clean towels, said she would get him a key the next day, and said goodnight to him. She would tell Nicole,

Rachel, and Linda the next day which would be Saturday when everyone would sleep late.

The following morning, Tina went to Meghan's room, not understanding at all. "Mom, you know Nicole wanted Mark's room." *What was she thinking*? Meghan tried to explain a few things to Tina, in love.

"I need to be there for Nick, and not treat him badly. Everything will work out."

Tina walks away looking somewhat sad.

That Saturday morning, not being able to sleep Meghan was up making coffee when Nick walks in.

"I just want to thank you for helping me out."

"No problem."

Meghan really wanted to ask, *Where are all your other men and women now*? In the back of her mind was her mother's voice again saying, *If you just hold your peace, and let the Lord fight your battles. Vengeance belongs to God and that the battle belongs to Him. Her Mama was always right. Meghan was just thinking that their dad really paid for the way he treated their mother, before he left this world.*

Meghan's mom left him and the woman he was dating poisoned him. It was as if karma is a BITCH.

"Would you like something to eat," Nick asked Meghan.

"No, I'm straight. Thank you though."

"I'll cook," Nick said.

She thought of *how she used to love for him to cook for her*. But that was a very long time ago. After they broke up, and had gotten on speaking terms again, she had gone to his house for dinner parties a few times. There were always some woman or man there cooking with Nick.

"No, I'm just having coffee. I will get something later, maybe after the kids are up."

"How is Mark these days?"

"He is holding his own. He has a 4.75 GPA. There are times he calls too much, just to check on me."

"WHAT! That's great. He was always a book worm."

"Yes, he is smart. He wants to become a doctor."

"Look Meghan, I will help you with the bills. I know they will be pulling my car any day now."

Meghan was thinking. *It is true. What goes around comes around.* When Nick walked out on her, she lost everything, including her car. There were times it was so cold and windy outside while waiting on the bus, she would have tears in her eyes. To top it off, she would have to walk from her house to downtown Harvey. If not, her transfer would run out, and she would have to walk from thirty-fifth Street and the Dan Ryan to the Mechanize hospital. She was determined to make it.

As thoughts of her struggle was running through her mind, Rachel, Nicole, Tina, and Linda were up and had come to the kitchen. Linda just looked at Nick as if to say, *What the hell are you doing here?* The girls just acted as if it was a normal day. Nick had to feel very uncomfortable at this point, but Meghan also acted as if this was just a normal day at home.

Linda starts fixing bacon and eggs for everyone. Nick ate with them. Meghan only had a few bites, and excused herself. She knew Mark was going to call soon, and she wanted to get to the phone before anyone else. By the time she got to her bedroom the phone rang, and she quickly answered.

"Mom, how are you?" Mark's voice came through loud and clear.

"I'm fine baby, what about you?"

"I have lots of homework."

"You can do it. You know you can. Mark, there is something I need to tell you."

"Is it about your health?"

"No. I wanted you to hear this from me. Nick is here. Someone robbed him over the Labor Day weekend while he was out of town. He showed up at my door. He had no place else to go."

"How long will he be staying?"

"I'm not sure."

"Well Mom, it's up to you."

"Mark he's in your room."

"My room?"

"Yes, baby, you know that's the only empty bedroom."

"Nick wouldn't be in my room," Meghan said, trying not to sound sarcastic."

"I know mom. It's okay."

"Mom?"

"Yes, baby?"

"If I had any doubt about God, you just renewed it. You went through a lot of hardship because of that man. I'm not sure I could forgive him, and let him move in."

"I know Mark. It's not me. It is God working in me."

The conversation soon ended, and by that time Nicole was at her door.

"Mom, you know Nick would not have given you a place to live if you were homeless."

"But what have I always told you, baby? Treat people the way you want to be treated. I let God pay me, and I let God pay Nick. I cannot teach you one thing in words, and show you the opposite with my actions. I want you to know that God is real, and that He is real in me."

Nicole returned to the kitchen where Rachel, Linda and Tina were sitting. Nick had gone back to the attic.

Nick could not understand how Meghan was willing to help him, after the way he had treated her. She really was one of a kind. He had treated her dirty. Actually, he was ashamed of himself. She was now living with this HIV shit because of him. The only good thing about this situation was that they did not get a divorce. That way if Meghan did outlive him, she would get all of his death insurance, and would also get his widow's benefits. If not, the kids would get all of that. He made sure of that. He included them in his will.

Meghan came back into the room. They had made plans to have a girl's day out at the Mall, so she told them to get ready.

Linda spoke first, "You mean you're going to leave Nick in your house?"

"Linda, he's a whore not a thief. You know that." she said smiling.

"I guess you're right, but I'm still locking my door."

"So am I."

They both laughed out loud and returned to their bedrooms.

Each came out dressed casually. By this time, Nick was sitting there watching TV. He took one look at Meghan and just dropped his head. Meghan looked good really good. She had made it a point to look that way. She gave him a look, as if to ask, *You're not going out?*

As if reading her mind Nick says, "I have no place to go, and friends are few these days."

Meghan knew, word had gotten around that he was infected. She worked with one of his associates that made the comment, "Girl, you don't want Nick back." That was all that was said, but Meghan knew what he meant by that statement.

"Well, you ladies have fun. Try not to spend all your money in one place."

"You're not going to take it with you when you die," Linda said.

Nick muttered in a low voice, "You're right about that."

It was a good day over all for the ladies. They really made the best of it. Meghan drove in her car to North Riverside Shopping Mall, located on Cermak Road. They shopped and ate lunch, and then continued with more shopping.

The big purchase of the day was to be Nicole's prom dress. It was a beautiful black dress, a 'one of a kind'. Yeah, right! She had seen Vanna White wearing it on The Wheel of Fortune. She had promised to keep up her grades, or the dress would be taken away before the prom.

Rachel and Tina were each granted an item of their own choice. Meghan bought a piece of jewelry, and Linda bought a dressy party dress.

Thank God for the comfortable shoes they all wore. On the way back home, they all realized they were happy and tired. After reaching home, all they wanted to do was shower and go to bed. Even the girls were ready to sleep.

Nick was already in his room when they returned.

NICK'S DOWNFALL

Two months later, Nick's car was repossessed, and he had no way to get to work. His job was fifteen miles from Meghan's house, thirty miles round trip. Nick had to ask Meghan if she could give him a ride. This was a reminder of how Meghan must have felt when he left her, and her car was repossessed. He felt like dirt again, knowing he treated her the way he did. *Wishing, wishing, wishing*! No matter how he wished, he could not go back and change the past.

Meghan looked up and said, "Yes, I'll get up an hour earlier and drop you off. Do you think you can get a ride back to the city?"

"Yes, yes, I can," Nick said fast.

This went on for three months. It really took a toll on Meghan. But Nick could not get a car because his credit was so bad.

Mark was graduating from college. The pharmaceutical company that hired him also gave him a new car. Mark still had the car Meghan got him after his high school graduation. He agreed to sell it to Nick.

As time went on it was hard for Nick to pay Mark. Nick didn't say his check was garnished each paycheck $500.00. He had to work lots of over time just to make ends meet. Nick having the car was a blessing on Meghan.

When Nick was living the good life, he had lots of friends. But now it seemed the only person that was willing to help him was Meghan. Now he could remember something his dear mother had tried to tell him once. *Treat people the way you want to be treated, and do not burn your bridges. You might have to cross them again.*

Nick could not understand why Meghan was so nice to him. Why could not he see what he had in her before he mistreated her? She was worth more than what he chose over her, many times more. Again *wishing, wishing, wishing*, no amount of wishing could change the past.

And yet Nick did realize that she was a good woman, but he was not really the man she needed. He was not the confident man she deserved. He always listened to his sorry ass friends ... they always had something negative to say about her.

Some of the times when Meghan came in from work, she looked so tired. Nick knew she was working extra hours to maintain her obligations.

After two years, Nick said he was moving. He thanked Meghan, and told her that he found a one-bedroom apartment. Linda and the girls jumped for joy!

Meghan just said, "Okay, if you think you can afford it." She knew they both had gotten some of their bills paid off.

That summer Nick moved into his own apartment. Everything seemed to be going good for him.

Then, Meghan was at work one day in November when Rachel called very upset!

"Mom...." Meghan's heart stopped beating. "Mom...."

"Rachel, what's wrong?"

"They are putting Nick's stuff outside."

"What do you mean?"

"There are men putting his furniture outside!"

"OH MY GOD," said Meghan to Rachel. "Okay, I'll call you right back."

Nick's apartment was near them, between the school and Meghan's house.

She called Nick. Before she could get any words out, Nick said, "Yes, I know."

"Why didn't you say something?"

"Meghan, you have done enough for me. I just couldn't ask."

"Meghan hung up, called a few friends, and they went over to move Nick's stuff back to her house. Meghan knew Nick had gone out and got some very nice furniture. He always went for the best. That day Meghan went home early. Nick came after work.

Meghan asked him again, "Why didn't you call me?"

"I just can't seem to get it together," Nick stated, looking lost.

Meghan could tell by looking at him, Nick's health was failing more by the day. After moving him back in for the second time, each day Nick seemed to get weaker and weaker. He was taking off time from work. Meghan tried to talk him into going to the doctor, but he would always give some kind of excuse. He did not want to admit how sick he was.

In all this time, not once had she seen Tyler for any more than to say hello. Tyler understood Meghan wasn't going to date him with Nick in the house. He respected her for that, and for so many other things. *How could she show so much love for that Nick, who had been so nasty to her*? He wondered.

NICK'S LAST DAYS

Meghan was spreading herself thin trying to care for him and her kids. Nick worked as long as he could. About six months later he became so sick he had to go into a nursing home. She tried to see him after work every day.

Nick died three months later, nine days after his birthday. Meghan made sure he had a very nice birthday party at home.

*   *   *

Meghan's grandparents had not said anything to her about Meghan's health. But they had gotten wind of what was going on from Linda. During this same time, Grandma Pearl was getting sicker and sicker. Meghan had called every week, but really could not get down to Mississippi to see them. Tyler had offered a few times to take her. Once Meghan had agreed, and she paid for everything. This was so there would not be any kind of a misunderstanding on his part, about her sleeping with him.

Grandma Pearl had commented that she didn't look as happy as she did a few years earlier. Meghan would not talk about it.

She just said, "Now look, I came to see you, not for you to worry about me."

A short time after that, Grandma Pearl was put into a nursing home in New Orleans. She would be near two of her daughters who lived there Maryann and Sara. The family decided to put Grandma Pearl in a nursing home there because her illness turned for the worst. Meghan never saw her alive again. Grandma Pearl died a year later. Meghan did not let Tyler go with her to the funeral. The last time, Tyler went south with her they got into a heated argument about sex. She had told him to stay away from her. Meghan made up her mind that this would not be only a sexual relationship....

Meghan took Grandma Pearl's death very hard, and it affected her. She lost weight and just really went down in her appearance. Mark, Linda, and the girls were worried about her health. To Meghan, it seemed that the good people in her life were leaving her. And now she had this HIV running around in her body just waiting to kill her someday.

*   *   *

Grandpa Willie lasted two years after Grandma Pearl died. During that time, Meghan went to Mississippi with her uncle Kenneth (one of her mother's brothers) to see Grandpa Willie once or twice every three months. Meghan made sure to talk to him daily and sent him nice gifts.

A few times Meghan even asked Tyler to come along. But the last time he went, they had a really bad argument, and Meghan told him she never wanted to see him again. Uncle Kenneth and Tyler were like two peas in a pot. They are around the same age. Uncle Ken would invite Tyler even if Meghan did not agree.

The last time she saw Grandpa Willie alive he wanted her to talk to her cousin Janet. Meghan knew that was the last time she would see him alive. Grandpa Willie had that same look Meghan had seen so many times before. It's called the look of death!

"Meg, I want you to do the best you can. You will make a lot of mistakes along the way, but you ask God to forgive you and He will. People will kick you if they can, but God is a forgiving God. Do your best, baby." With that he went to sleep.

Meghan kept her promise and went to see her crazy cousin. Her mother's sister's daughter Janet was a little mental, so the family stayed away from her.

Grandpa Willie died two weeks later. Meghan took a plane to the funeral. Tyler came with his cousin Rhonda. Meghan did not want to be around him at all, but her family loved him.

AFTER RETURNING TO CHICAGO

Tyler called Meghan. "Meghan, can you meet me today? We really need to talk."

"Okay I will meet you at Rudy's Place at 4:30 pm."

They were both there on time. After they were seated, Tyler spoke first.

"Meghan it's been six years. Both of us have been through pure hell, alone and together. What do I have to do to make you understand that I will always be here for you? There was no response from Meghan.

"I told you the first night we met you would be mine. Will it take another six years for you to realize we belong together. Hell, by that time, I will be too old to chew butter!" They both had to laugh behind that.

"Tyler there has been too much happening in my life. I know you have other lovers, and me dealing with this illness. And besides, I've had others also.

Tyler knew that was a lie. He knew Meghan had not dated anyone in the past six years. Linda kept him updated. She could not keep secrets from Tyler about Meghan.

"With that, what are you trying to tell me, that your feelings have changed?" Tyler also knew Meghan was worried about him since Betty's death five years ago.

"If you can look me in my eyes and tell me that you don't want me after all these years, I will leave and never bother you again.

Meghan, you know at my age, in another fifteen years I will need Viagra to keep up with you."

"I have been known to raise the dead. That's right!" she said with a smile.

"Well, if my memory serves me right you are pretty good at it too."

Meghan starts blushing and forgot she was mad at Tyler then said, "Tyler, Betty has only been dead five years."

"Meghan, do you think she's on a trip, and will be returning any day?"

"No, let's just give it a little more time."

"Then, will you marry me?"

"We will talk about it. Deal?"

He went in his pocket and pulled out a lovely black box. He opened it. The diamond almost blinded her. *God it was beautiful*! She thought.

"Tyler … when, where, and how? How long have you had this?"

"For two months after Betty died."

"Did you buy it for me?"

"For you! Who are you? Meghan, who else would I buy it for?"

"Why didn't you tell me that day we talked?"

"Because I wanted to make sure you still felt the same way. Now look me in my eyes; tell me you don't love me."

"Ty," she dropped her eyes then she started thinking about how she acted a fool over the years.

"No, Meghan, look at me!"

Meghan looks into Tyler's eyes and says, "Tyler, I have always loved you just as much as the first night I met you. There is something you must understand. I am an advocate for women living with HIV/Aids who were infected by their mates. My face is known by many."

"So, what! They're not marrying you … I am! My family knows all about you, and your work."

They stood there staring at each other. Tyler spoke. "We are going to do this openly, not secretively. I want you to start wearing this ring today."

Meghan just responded by crying and saying, "YES, YES!"

THE WEDDING DAY

Mark was handsome, confident, and all smiles the day he walked his mother down the aisle to give her to Tyler. He and his sisters felt that he had never stopped being a friend of the family, and that he was a good man. They were glad to gain him as a stepfather.

At that point Meghan knew of some possibilities. She knew that something good could come out of pain.

Ida Byther-Smith
Biography

Ida Byther-Smith received her AAS at Malcom X College and her BA from Governors State University.

She has done numerous television interviews and appeared in articles in Ebony Magazine, POZ Magazine, Chicago Tribune, Chicago Sun-Times, and Chicago Defender. She speaks as an advocate for those living with HIV with compassion that only comes through personal experience.

Ida worked especially with church groups and people over 50 to get the message of valuing yourself and walking in courage for those who often feel misused and ashamed.

Although we do not hear much about HIV/Aids, it is still prevalent. Ida has been infected with HIV for 30 years and 20 years with Aids. She has become a living testimony that one can survive with the proper treatment.

One of her major goals is to disseminate information to women about the HIV/Aids epidemic since women face special risks and are still getting infected because of their lack of knowledge.